BEING
SOBER
AND BECOMING
HAPPY

*The Best Ideas from The Director
of Spiritual Guidance at Hazelden*

Dr. John A. MacDougall

Credits
Photography by Verna Pitts Photography www.vernapittsphotography.com
Custom Suit by Simpson Sim of Hong Kong
Tie by Leonard, Paris
Shoes by Louis Vuitton, Paris

ISBN: 0615847374
ISBN 13: 978-0615847375
Library of Congress Control Number: 2013913005
CreateSpace Independent Publishing Platform
North Charleston, SC

ACKNOWLEDGMENTS

I'm John MacDougall, and I wrote this book. As the author, I am solely responsible for its content.

I work at the Hazelden residential treatment center in Center City, Minnesota, as the director of spiritual guidance and have been there since 1994.

Hazelden helps individuals, families, and communities struggling with alcohol abuse, substance abuse, and drug addiction transform their lives. Its locations across the United States help people at all stages of the treatment and recovery process, supporting them with the Twelve Step-based model that is the modern standard for addiction treatment and recovery services. In addition, Hazelden provides professional education and addiction research and engages in addiction awareness and public-policy activities. Hazelden also has a publishing division, but this is not a Hazelden book, and Hazelden has not endorsed this book.

This book contains illustrative examples drawn from patients, from people in the parishes I served as pastor, and from people I have met in the rooms of Alcoholics Anonymous. The details have been changed so they cannot be recognized from the stories in this book. If you think you can recognize someone, please be assured that you cannot.

In this book, I write extensively about the fellowships of Alcoholics Anonymous and Narcotics Anonymous, and I quote from the "Big Book," *Alcoholics Anonymous*. I quote from the Big Book because it is still the best thing that has ever been written on the subject of recovery from alcoholism. I wholeheartedly endorse the fellowships of Alcoholics

Anonymous, Narcotics Anonymous, Al-Anon, Gamblers Anonymous, and the other groups that have put the Twelve Steps to work to restore their members to sanity. I endorse them, but they don't endorse me. I am not writing this book as a member of any fellowship or as a spokesperson for any fellowship. My words are my own.

My hope is that this book will be useful to you, the reader, in your recovery. I have been helping alcoholics and addicts get and stay sober at Hazelden for 19 years, and this book is an attempt to share my ideas with a wider audience. My hope is that, from the many ideas in this book, there will be a few that provide you with some lasting value. —John M.

CONTENTS

INTRODUCTION

My hope in writing Being Sober and Becoming Happy is to provide an accessible guide to maintaining the sobriety the reader already has over the lifetime, and becoming happy over time. In thinking about readers, I imagine three groups of people: recovering alcoholics and addicts, people who are in relationships with recovering alcoholics and addicts, and people who work professionally with alcoholics and addicts.

For recovering people, the book begins with the most basic goal: staying sober. It covers the behaviors that are necessary to maintain long-term sobriety in the Twelve Step programs, which are the method of recovery that has the best outcomes. The chapters on Surrender and Trust, and Practice These Principles go into more detail on what we need to do to extend and protect our sobriety.

There is a chapter on spiritual recovery from trauma and abuse, because almost half of the people in the recovering community have some childhood experiences of trauma or abuse. Some have already recovered, and some will need more help in order to stay sober.

At this point, the book takes a turn and heads towards the things that allow for happiness. It examines healthy love and romance, and the sources of resilient hope. The book continues with examples of finding joy in life, in part by using the traditions of the Twelve Step programs.

The final chapter, "Becoming Happy" finds its origin in the well loved "Twelve Promises" of A.A. In that chapter, I reflect on how they actually come true in our lives and we end up happy when we take the Twelve Steps and Twelve Traditions, and do them.

For people in relationships with recovering persons, this book can be useful, if you read it for yourself, and not for them. This is the same idea that brought Al-Anon into existence. Al-Anon is a Twelve Step program for relatives and friends of alcoholics. Al-Anon teaches us to practice the Twelve Steps for ourselves, so that we can have a parallel program of recovery, parallel to the recovery of those we love.

For professionals, this book can give insight into how the Twelve Step programs actually work to bring about change. We professionals may already be referring alcoholics and addicts to these programs, but mere attendance doesn't bring about change. If simply sitting in the rooms of A.A. or NA brought about recovery, then with all the time I have spent in hospitals, I should be a surgeon by now. We recover by taking the steps, by carrying out the traditions, and by practicing the spiritual principles in all our affairs. Even the bumper stickers help: "Live and Let Live", "One Day at a Time", and "Let Go and Let God."

My hope is that this book will be helpful to you, the reader, in your recovery, your relationships, or your work. If it is, then I will have achieved my goal. My suggestion is that you take the book with an Al-Anon attitude of "take what you like, and leave the rest."

John A. MacDougall

CHAPTER 1:

STAYING SOBER

WHY WE DRINK

We drink because we have a biological disease called alcoholism. It is a biological disease that has a spiritual solution. This doesn't make much sense, but very little about addiction makes sense. It is an entirely irrational disease. Our midbrains, where the disease lives, will never change. Recovery appears to live in the limbic system of the brain, which is the home of music, poetry, spirituality, and love. We ultimately stay sober in a fellowship of men and women who share their experience, strength, and hope in order to stay sober and to help other alcoholics achieve sobriety. That fellowship is A.A.

For us alcoholics to stay sober, it helps to understand our disease and to know why we drink. We drink because we are alcoholics. That's it. There really are no other reasons. There are other details, but not other reasons. We are all different in that we have different details, but we are all the same in that we all have the same disease. The disease is addiction. Alcoholism is simply addiction to alcohol.

Some of my details make recovery harder: I was a battered child. I have a "dual diagnosis" of post-traumatic stress disorder, as well as alcoholism. I have chronic pain. Some of my details make recovery easier: I am an economically secure white male living in America, so I don't suffer from discrimination or oppression. My drinking isn't caused by my problems, and it isn't relieved by the opportunities I get.

All of us alcoholics and addicts are essentially the same. Each drug is different. Some addictive drugs are uppers, some are downers, some make us numb, some make us romantic, some make us argumentative, some make us dreamy, some make us lack initiative, and some make us obsessively busy. But what all addictive drugs have in common is that they gradually take over our lives, crowding out every other loyalty—God, other people, work, patriotism, avocations, love—and our lives focus more and more on obtaining our drugs, using them, rebounding from our use of them, and planning how to do them again.

Our disease of addiction is chronic, meaning it does not go away; progressive, in that it gets worse; and fatal. We don't just have a "drinking problem," we *are* alcoholics. Our addiction to alcohol becomes the core of who we are.

Because we are alcoholics, the most natural thing in the world to do is drink. Every day, even though I am well established in recovery, the most natural thing in the world for me to do is drink. Even though I have had over twenty-four years of staying sober every single day, it will never become natural. The natural thing for me to do today is drink. Why? How?

When I try to explain this to normal people, or the "earth people," as I call them, I tell a fictional story that is true, even if it isn't exactly factual. It represents what has always been going on.

When I was in my twenties, I would go to a restaurant for lunch with a friend. I didn't know I was developing into an alcoholic, and he didn't know that he wasn't. We were already different. What was different about us was that I had one button in my brain on the subject of drinking. That button was labeled "more." He had two buttons. His were labeled "more" and "enough."

The waitress comes and asks, "Would you gentlemen like a drink?" "Yes" (my hand shoots up). My friend hesitates, but then after a moment says, "Yes, thank you, I'll have a drink." She brings two drinks, and we drink them. After ten minutes, she comes back. "Would you gentlemen like another?" "Yes," I respond immediately. I only have one button in my brain. It says "more," and I push it.

He hesitates. I am thinking, *My, you're slow*. Then he says, "Yes, thank you, I'll have another." She brings two drinks, and we drink them.

Twenty minutes later, she comes back. "Would you gentlemen like another?" "Yes," I say; my hand shoots up. He's hesitating even longer. Now I know he's really slow. Finally, he speaks. "No, thank you," he says, "I've had…" (he pushes the button I don't have) "…enough." She brings one drink. I drink it quickly.

I'm thinking about my friend: *What's wrong with you? Why did you say no? We're not out of time. They're not out of liquor. We're not out of money. That's all the reasons there are to say no. Why did you say no? I don't get it!* He's thinking, *My, you certainly have a sense of urgency about your drinks!* But we are polite, and neither of us says anything to the other, and life goes on. We are, however, already on different life paths. I am developing an addiction to alcohol, and he is not. Our life situations are the same, but our bodies and minds are different. I am an alcoholic, and he is not. I am just not showing very many symptoms of my disease yet. It will take a while before I am "seriously alcoholic."

It took a long time before I realized I was "seriously alcoholic." We each have our own paths and our own stories as we move toward the First Step of Alcoholics Anonymous, where we admit we are powerless over alcohol and our lives have become unmanageable. Again, the details vary, but we must fully understand this about ourselves.

Years ago, there was a television police drama called *Hill Street Blues*. Every episode opened the same way: a roll call of officers and a briefing about the day's events led by a sergeant named Phil. Each week, as the briefing was ending and the officers rose to leave the room, Phil would interrupt them by pointing at them and shouting: "And hey. HEY! Be careful out there!"

I adapted that as my Step One reminder. I am not a morning person. I do not spring from bed, ready to greet the bright new day. I get up slowly and grudgingly. On awakening, before I open my eyes, I say to myself, in that same voice that Sergeant Phil had, "Good morning, John. You are an alcoholic. Pay attention!" Oh, that's right! I'm still an alcoholic! It didn't go away overnight. In fact, in my sleep, the reset button was pushed in my brain, and I wake up alcoholic. It is my recovery that went away while I was sleeping, not my alcoholism. I wake up in my natural state of alcoholism, not in my artificial state of recovery. I have to make a conscious choice to be in recovery today, or else my natural state of alcoholism will take over and I will be likely to drink—because that's what alcoholics do!

WHAT TO DO ABOUT IT

When my fellow alcoholics relapse, I never ask them why. I know why. There may be some event that happened at the same time as the relapse, but the event is a detail. We relapse because we are alcoholics, and relapsing is what we do unless we have a program, peers, sponsors, steps, and a Higher Power.

The best thing ever written about alcoholism is still chapter 5 of A.A.'s Big Book. It's called "How It Works," and that's what it is about. The opening is read at every A.A. meeting. The conclusion of that reading speaks of "three pertinent ideas":

(a) That we were alcoholic and could not manage our own lives.
(b) That probably no human power could have relieved our alcoholism.
(c) That God could and would if He were sought. (p. 60)

We learn to take the Twelve Steps to get sober, and we learn to keep coming back to meetings to stay sober. There is one difficulty with this method: the disease itself keeps strengthening over time. We achieve a certain level of spiritual awareness in our initial round of the Twelve Steps, and that is sufficient to get us sober. If we simply do what we did to get sober, we will have trouble staying sober over the long term because, as I said, the disease itself strengthens over time. Think of the Twelve Steps as spiritual medicine. The "dose" of spirituality that is enough to get us sober isn't high enough to keep us sober as the years go by because the underlying disease of addiction gets stronger, not weaker. As the disease gets stronger, we need a higher "dose" of spirituality to beat the disease.

How do we know this is true? How do we know the disease of alcoholism gets stronger? Two ways: When alcoholics are sober for many years and then pick up drinking again, they do not start back at the beginning of their drinking career with little colored drinks with parasols in them or with apple wine. No. They rocket past their previous drinking levels within a few weeks and drink a whole lot more. The disease has gotten much stronger, even while the alcoholic was not drinking at all, and the drinking level will soar to catch up with the disease. Secondly, if the alcoholic has had seven or more years of sobriety and then goes out binge-drinking, the withdrawal symptoms will not be what they used to be. The withdrawal symptoms are likely to be what they would have been if the alcoholic had been drinking the whole time.

So, for example, at the end of my binges twenty-four years ago, I used to sweat, shake, and throw up. If I drank for a month or so now and tried to dry out on my own, I would be likely to sweat, shake, throw up, and have a seizure—if I was lucky. If I was unlucky, I'd also have a heart arrhythmia. And if the arrhythmia was arrhythmic enough, my heart might stop entirely, and I'd die.

Many alcoholics get sober and find that both the symptoms and consequences of addiction go away. We aren't craving alcohol, we aren't drinking alcohol, and it isn't running our lives. We aren't having financial problems, legal problems, relationship problems, or medical problems. We are free to imagine that the disease has gone away because both the symptoms and the consequences have gone away. Life is good. But because addiction is a chronic disease, it hasn't gone away. It has gone into remission. We have had treatment or we are going to a Twelve Step program or we are in some other program of spiritual connection or personal growth, and the "dose" of spirituality is enough to push the disease of addiction into remission. We are all right, for now.

Staying sober over time requires an increasing "dose" of spirituality over time, because this disease grows on us. The Big Book of A.A. explains it this way:

> It is easy to let up on the spiritual program of action and rest on our laurels. We are headed for trouble if we do, for alcohol is a subtle foe. We are not cured of alcoholism. What we really have is a daily reprieve contingent on the maintenance of our spiritual condition. Every day is a day when we must carry the vision of God's will into all of our activities. (p. 85)

I have already decided that I am an alcoholic and that I will pay attention. To what shall I pay attention so I can stay sober over the long term? I will pay attention to the maintenance of my spiritual condition. We have all heard, "It's a spiritual program." If so, then it is our spiritual condition that will keep us sober. How can we do this?

SPIRITUAL FITNESS

If we are spiritually fit, we will not relapse. If we turn our wills and our lives over to the care of God, as we understand God, we are granted a daily reprieve from relapse.

We begin with a daily commitment to our program of recovery. Mine is very short. "Good morning, John. You're an alcoholic. Pay attention!" Then, once I am up, I ask God that my motives be divorced from selfish, self-seeking, and dishonest motives, as the Big Book describes on page 86. As I write this, I am sixty-four years old. I have already made a lot of the available mistakes. As a result, when I do something wrong, it is often not a mistake—it is on purpose. I do it not by accident but because I had the wrong motive: I wanted to get away with something. I wanted to be a smartass. I wanted to get something that was not rightfully mine. I wanted to express a character defect instead of practicing the principles of the program. So, if I pray for the right motives, the right actions will probably follow. I pray for the right motives before I have met anyone that day so that I am more likely to be guided by God's will than self-will.

We all find our own way to begin the day with commitment to our program of recovery. Many people take time to read from the *Twenty-Four Hours a Day* book or another meditation book. Many people have a formal prayer. It is good to find a way to set our minds straight.

My favorite sentence in the Big Book is, "Rarely have we seen a person fail who has thoroughly followed our path." If we start on our path first thing in the morning every day, we are likely to follow it.

In 1989, I tapered down on my drug use and drinking to the point at which I could safely stop and then went to A.A. on a day when I had not yet had a drink or a drug. I raised my hand and said, "Hi. I'm John, and I'm an alcoholic." They said "Hi, John." I had already identified a man who I wanted to be my sponsor, and I asked him. He said he had two questions for me: "Do you have the desire to stop drinking?" I said yes. "Are you willing to do what you're told?" I said yes. He gave me a Big Book and said, "This is a Big Book." I thought, *That's kind of basic.* He opened it and said, "It's in black and white.

Read the black part." He went on to say, "If you read chapters five and six, 'How It Works' and 'Into Action,' and you do what they say, you will never drink or use again."

At that point, I had been drinking and taking drugs every day, every hour of every day, for thirty years: from first awakening to the moment I slammed myself to sleep with Jack Daniels, Valium, and Percodan. Somehow I knew what he said was true. I had detoxed myself, and I didn't want to go back. I read the book, I did what it said, and I never had a drink or a drug again.

My story is highly unusual in that I detoxed myself and never had a relapse, and I intend no criticism of anyone whose story is different. It makes no difference how many times we relapse. The alcoholic who has never relapsed and the alcoholic who has relapsed many times wake up absolutely equal. We all wake up as alcoholics, and we all need to turn our wills and our lives over to the care of God, as we understand God, every day. What we did yesterday does not count. What we might do tomorrow is a fantasy. We all need to take the first step and recommit to sobriety right now. Right now is all we have.

TURNING IT OVER

To be sober, we need to turn our wills and our lives over to God's care with complete abandon.

I have a mental image of complete abandon. In 1979, I joined a volunteer fire department in southern New Jersey. In the training, we were supposed to learn a technique called "riding the rails." It was a method for going down a ladder very fast in a crisis. You wrap your ankles around the rails and slide fast, missing the rungs. It looked scary, and I avoided the training. A year later, I was fighting a fire inside an old, decrepit apartment building on the second floor. I had a heavy turnout coat, helmet, air pack, and hose, and a partner in the room. Suddenly there was a back draft, and the room filled with flames. My partner smashed out the window and went down a ladder, riding the rails. The flames chased me right out after him. I wrapped my ankles around the rails and hurtled to the ground with complete abandon. I hit really hard, fell on my back, and ended up black and blue, but I wasn't burned. That's what I think of when I read the phrase "complete abandon." I was totally committed to going out that window—and I need to be totally committed to God's care.

Spiritual fitness remains forever our goal because it is a daily reprieve from our natural state of drunkenness. We don't arrive at spiritual fitness by meditating entirely on what is good, but by admitting our own weakness.

WE ARE NOT GOD

To be sober, we start by recognizing that we are not God. That sounds absurdly simple, but the truth is that when I was drinking and drugging, I behaved as if I were God. My voice was the only voice I listened to. My will was the only will I acted on. My view of what was right was the only standard of right that I considered valuable. It never occurred to me that there was any standard in the world other than my own.

Sure, I knew there were laws, but they were OK because I approved of them. In fact, I thought of myself as a law-and-order man. I followed the law, and I approved of the law—no conflict there. Of course, I never considered the laws against drunk driving. That little discrepancy literally never crossed my mind. I was able to know that I was driving really drunk at times and that drunk driving was against the law and yet still believe that I never broke the law. I could have passed a lie-detector test on that point. This is easy to do if you are insane. Alcoholism is a form of insanity. With alcoholism, I could look straight at two contradictory facts, know they contradicted each other, and believe them both. It's easy when you have alcoholic insanity. Of course I was right, because I was the very definition of rightness. Whatever I had just done was, by definition, right. It was all so simple.

In early recovery, I learned the difference between justifying something and rationalizing it. I was at the Apple Computer store buying a laser printer that was, back then, expensive. The clerk asked how I wanted to pay for it, and I hesitated, explaining that I was trying to decide whether to charge it on American Express (and get the frequent flyer miles) or take the free financing from Apple. "Oh, good," he replied. "That way you can justify your decision now instead of trying to rationalize it later."

That's the difference. In recovery, we consider God's will for our lives, not just our own will. We try to figure out the just decision to make. When I was using, I would act on impulse, and then, when it didn't work, I would search for a reason why my actions were rational. I would try to "rationalize" my behavior.

As we realize we *have* a God, rather than that we *are* gods, we get to stop trying to *control* life and instead get to simply *live* life. I've decided my life is unmanageable only when I am trying to manage it. My life isn't meant to be managed—it is meant to be lived.

I used to cram as much as possible into my daily schedule and then try to manage it all. This put me in constant conflict with time, immovable objects, and other people. I then struggled for mastery over them all. You may have seen people like me in airports yelling at the ticket clerk about how *their* trip is terribly important and they *must* get there on time. They imagine that if they are loud and angry enough, America's air-travel system will cough up an extra airplane for them.

Today, in my work at Hazelden, I have a calendar, but I try to leave holes in it. Sometimes someone doesn't show up for an appointment. Instead of being mad that the person is wasting my time, I accept that it is an extra hole in my calendar. I leave my door open or go walking around. Many times God has something good for me to do that I wander across or that comes wandering by my office, something I never would have seen or known about if I were trying to be the master of my day.

WE ARE CHILDREN OF GOD

To stay sober, we accept ourselves as children of God, worthy of dignity, respect, and recovery. We have value because our Creator says so. I hear people say, "I have self-esteem problems." If we have self-esteem problems, then we don't know who we are. We are children of God. That idea is in the Bible, and it is also in the founding document of the United States, the Declaration of Independence.

It could be called the "Declaration of Resentments" because it is mostly a list of complaints against the King of England:

He has plundered our seas, ravaged our Coasts, burnt our towns, and destroyed the lives of our people. He is at this time transporting large Armies of foreign

Mercenaries to compleat the works of death, desolation and tyranny, already begun with circumstances of Cruelty & perfidy scarcely paralleled in the most barbarous ages, and totally unworthy the Head of a civilized nation.

But in the midst of this, we find a totally new idea, the idea of natural rights:

We hold these truths to be self-evident, that all men are created equal, that they are endowed by their Creator with certain unalienable Rights, that among these are Life, Liberty and the pursuit of Happiness.

I know the authors meant men, not women, and just white men, and only certain kinds of white men. But they got the idea going, and it has grown to include all people. So whether we take it from the Bible or the Declaration of Independence, we need to take it as true that we have a natural-born value as children of God.

ANONYMITY

To stay sober, we practice the spiritual principle of anonymity so we can attain spiritual freedom and leave our self-esteem problems behind. Tradition Twelve reads, "Anonymity is the spiritual foundation of all our Traditions, ever reminding us to place principles before personalities." This means we are equals in a fellowship of men and women, neither above nor below others. We do not change the way we act because of personal likes or dislikes, but act according to the principles of our program: honesty, openness, willingness, and fellowship.

Practicing the principle of anonymity may require the development of humility. Humility has nothing to do with humiliation. Humility means having a true, correct, and accurate view of ourselves. Once we understand that we are all children of God and that we all wake up as alcoholics and addicts who need to take the First Step today, then we will know we are equal.

Depending on our starting place, we may need to step up to become equal, or we may need to step down to become equal. We usually find it amusing when we see a grandiose person step down.

Another reason why anonymity is a vital spiritual survival tool is because there's a special, dangerous form of grandiosity. If I think I'm even 1 percent less likely to drink today than is the alcoholic living in a refrigerator box, that is grandiosity, because we both have the same brain disease. The disease itself will use that grandiosity against me in the form of complacency.

The principle of anonymity reminds me that we are, forever, all alike in our need for one another and our need for God and this program.

RESENTMENTS AND ACCEPTANCE

The Big Book of A.A. identifies resentments as the number one offender, killing more alcoholics than anything else. However, that was written when no one in A.A. had more than four years of sobriety. I believe that over the long run, complacency becomes the number one offender. The very fact that we have been sober a long time and our troubles are behind us is hijacked by the disease to tell us we don't have the disease any longer or we can now "handle it ourselves."

We learn to accept life on life's terms. We do not struggle to force people, places, or things to be different than they actually are. That means we accept life as it is, instead of forming a mental picture of how life should be and then measuring our lives against the arbitrary standard we have created.

Many alcoholics and addicts have a huge problem with resentments. We get stuck because we have a grievance against life for not meeting our expectations of how life should be. Many of us have used our resentments to rationalize our drinking. The hardest resentments to escape are the resentments caused by injustice—that is, incidents in life when we were the victims of injustice, when others were truly wrong and we were truly innocent victims.

When the lines between right and wrong are absolutely clear and they were wrong and we were right, we seemingly have no reason to give up our resentments. For example, I was a victim of terrible child abuse. So my abusers were guilty, and I was innocent. I had a bulletproof reason for resenting them.

My first sponsor said, "John, you have to kill your parents." I replied, "I've thought about it, but I don't want to do the time."

Then he said: "Not literally kill them, but you have to kill every expectation you have that they will ever love you. You go traveling a thousand miles with your beggar's bowl in your hands, hoping they will put some love in it, and they don't. Then you come away hurt and angry. Take your bowl somewhere else, where it can be filled. At this point in your life, their behavior has been completely consistent. They don't like you. It is not their behavior that is making you unhappy. It is your expectations that they should change. You need to lower your expectations to the point that they will be met, even if that level is nothing, nothing, nothing. Then they won't be able to make you unhappy."

It took me longer than a year to force my expectations all the way down to zero. At that time, I was already working at Hazelden, and I gave a patient lecture about once a week. A lot of the patients liked my lectures and would say something encouraging in the hallways when they saw me, but I would not listen to them. I refused to receive any affirmations. I realized that until my mother and father affirmed me, I was totally closed to anyone else affirming me. So I would go through life with no affirmation at all unless I changed my attitudes and perceptions.

I reclassified my parents as "ancestors." Everyone has ancestors, but they don't affect you as much as parents do. At the time of my mother's final illness, it turned out that the last thing she ever said to me was, "John, you can go to hell!" All I said was, "I know." It no longer mattered. I had stopped waiting for her.

When we resent someone or something, we think they are causing our resentments. But we are causing our own resentments with our expectations and our lack of acceptance. Acceptance is not approval. Acceptance is just the acceptance of reality. There will always be things in life we do not want to accept.

When we resent life and blame God, it is impossible to surrender to the care of God, because we are mad at God for the ways in which the world is unacceptable to us. For good reason the Serenity Prayer is the most popular prayer among recovering people:

God, grant me the serenity to accept the things I cannot change, the courage to change the things I can, and the wisdom to know the difference.

Acceptance is the key to all our problems today, and resentment—and the nurturing of our resentments—is the key to making all our problems forever unsolvable.

SURRENDER: LET GO AND LET GOD

To stay sober, we surrender to the care of our Higher Power. Defiance is our natural state as alcoholics and addicts. In defiance we surrender to the imaginary care of our chemicals. Recovery involves a revolution that frees us from our devotion to chemicals and makes us free to take on a new Higher Power. We should choose a Higher Power that is high enough to free us.

The disease itself throws up objections to God. Either we doubt that God exists or we find a bunch of grievances against God, or both. Only as alcoholics can we be so good at resentments that we can manage to resent a God we don't even believe in!

All of a sudden, when confronted with the chance to recover, alcoholics suddenly become moral philosophers. "How can I believe in a God who allows suffering?" "How can I believe in a God who requires faith as a condition of belief?" "If God is all powerful, then why didn't he just prevent my alcoholism in the first place?"

I've heard many of these questions. Then one day it dawned on me that I never subjected drinking to the same level of scrutiny: "Is Jack Daniels real? Does he sit on the porch in Lynchburg, Tennessee, personally overseeing every drop of whiskey? Is Captain Morgan a real pirate? And if so, why hasn't the navy caught him?"

I remember that in 1979 there was a batch of fake quaaludes in southern New Jersey that were actually fatally high doses of PCP. People who ingested one tablet died. People called them "killer 'ludes," and the price actually went up, because if one tablet killed you, then half a tablet must give you a really great high. We don't ask any of the tough questions about drugs.

When it comes to God, we have a lot of questions. What we don't have is a lot of answers. We don't need answers—we need a relationship.

Once a patient came up to me in the hallway at Hazelden and said, "John, I want to understand God." That's a lot to ask in a hallway conversation. I blurted out, "Forget it. Understanding is overrated." He asked, "What do you mean?" So I asked, "Do you like women?" He said yes. "Do you understand them?" He said no. "There you are!" I said. He got it.

I don't mean to blow off serious questions about good and evil. As a small child, I turned to God for help when I was being abused, but the abuse continued unchanged. I was not sophisticated enough to think about good and evil. I could only conclude that God would not help me.

There are three sources of bad things in life: randomness, error, and evil. Our beliefs need to accommodate all three. A car crosses the center line on the highway, and someone coming the other way is killed. Who gets killed? It's random. It's bad luck to be in that car. What was crossing the center line? It was an error. Every few weeks in America, we read a story about someone who takes a gun into a workplace and shoots several people because he or she has a grievance, then stops shooting only when the police shoot or capture the shooter. What is that? That is evil. These shooters have overwhelming anger and evil in their hearts.

In real life, we not only pay for our own mistakes; we sometimes pay consequences when we have done nothing wrong. There is no evidence that God steps in to stop all this. On the other hand, another body of evidence from men and women in recovery shows that when it was time for them to recover, their Higher Power stepped in and helped them do it. These two sets of evidence are contradictory.

What shall we do with this contradiction? God does not reliably intervene to prevent randomness, error, and evil, but God does seem to take care of us through times of hardship and addiction. My response is to minimize my exposure to randomness, error, and evil. I wear my seat belt, practice good health care, stay sober, and don't drive into bad neighborhoods at four a.m. to buy crack. I maximize my exposure to good things: I stick with my Twelve Step program; practice honesty, openness, and willingness; and have conscious contact with God so I am more likely to do the right thing.

To surrender, we take Step Three: "We made a decision to turn our will and our lives over to the care of God, *as we understood Him.*" I think of my will as my thoughts and my life as my actions. I invite God to guide what I think and what I do. It would be nice if I could make one big decision that lasts forever, but I have not been able to achieve that. What I have had to do is make a new decision each day and take one topic at a time.

After I greet the day with "Good morning, John, you're an alcoholic," I ask God for the right motives going forward. This is because if I have the right motives, the right actions will probably follow. Then I try to stay mentally in touch with the idea of God all day and mentally check in with the presence of God. Some Christians have had "WWJD" ("What would Jesus Do?") bracelets. They are trying to do the same thing. My question is aimed at God, not myself. It's, "What do you want me to do right now about this?" The more that question is on my mind, the better the day goes, and the happier I am.

When I live with this question, I can live without excuses and without blame. Things are what they are. I am an alcoholic. It's not anyone's fault. It's not an excuse for anything. It just is. When we surrender to our Higher Power, we can truly "live and let live" and commit ourselves to God's care.

I think back to 1968 when I made my first attempt at college. I was headed straight for failure because of my heavy drinking and drug use. I was eighteen years old and dating an eighteen-year-old girl. She was sweet and kind and everything I wanted. I was too drunk to even know if she knew she was dating me, but I thought I was dating her. We spent time together at the campus Christian fellowship house. Just before the break for the long Thanksgiving weekend, when she was going home for a few days, I was trying to talk to her about the future. She said, "I do not know what the future holds. I only know that God holds the future." It wasn't a cliché when she said it. She had such uncomplicated faith in God that it made me wish I had her faith.

She went home. Over the Thanksgiving break, she borrowed her brother's new Corvette Stingray and took it out on the Massachusetts Turnpike for a spin. She flipped the car and died in the crash. I was devastated, or thought I was, and quickly tried to drown my sorrows. I think of her from time to time, confident that God is caring for her. She is an image in my mind of turning our wills and our lives over to the care of God. She wasn't kept from crashing, but I am somehow sure she is OK and at home with God.

TRUST

To be sober, we trust God, and the program of recovery, for a positive result to our lives. We fulfill our responsibilities and trust God for the outcome of our efforts. We no longer have the burden of self-reliance.

One persistent delusion of addiction is "Don't worry—I can handle it!" First, our disease of addiction tells us we are not sick at all, and then, when we can no longer deny our illness, it tells us we can handle it alone. The fact is that quitting drinking and drugging is easy. I've done it several dozen times. Quitting is entirely different from getting and staying sober.

I like to point out the absurdity of handling our addictions alone by pointing out that we don't do *anything* important alone. I'm writing this sentence in an airplane on the way to Florida. I didn't build the airplane. I'm not piloting it. I didn't design or build my AirMac computer. I didn't knit my clothes. I didn't grow the food for the breakfast they just served. I can't distill gasoline or jet fuel. I have no idea even how to make a pencil from scratch. I don't do anything all by myself. For every single need I have during the day, I rely on a network of people. Now, all of a sudden, I am going to do my recovery all by myself? Why? How? I am trusting the Delta Airlines management, the Airline Pilots Association, and the Federal Aviation Administration this morning, and I haven't seen any of them. It's not that hard to trust God, because I have twenty-four years of sobriety as evidence that trusting God is working.

Trusting God can be a big relief, because if I trust God, then I don't have to *be* God. If there is no God, then I had better be a real expert at everything, be right all the time, and monitor everything all the time. Now that I have faith, I can "let go and let God."

One practical result is that I don't experience burnout at work at Hazelden, which some people do. Burnout is also called "compassion fatigue." This happens to clinicians who really care about the alcoholics and addicts in treatment. They burn out not from caring too much but from believing that the patient's recovery depends on them. When the patient shows signs of not recovering, or resisting recovery, the clinician tries harder and harder to get the patient well because the patient's recovery is riding on their shoulders. Then, if the patient relapses, the clinician is defeated.

I don't experience burnout because I know God is in charge, not me. I am responsible for my best effort every day, but I cannot control the outcome. I trust God to look after the patient, in treatment and afterward. I agree with A.A.'s "three pertinent ideas":

(a) That we were alcoholic and could not manage our own lives.
(b) That probably no human power could have relieved our alcoholism.
(c) That God could and would if He were sought.
(*Alcoholics Anonymous*, p. 60)

I am happy to be a human power who points people toward a real solution. If I were relying on just myself to treat addiction, it would be a terrible burden, because I would be solely responsible for the outcome. I don't know how I would handle the responsibility. Yes, I am part of a team, but when I meet with patients, it's one-on-one. I leave spaces in my schedule and leave my door open so God can put people in my path who need to talk with me, and I read every word in each patient's chart, looking for images and metaphors that might add up to a special insight for the patient when we meet. Then I trust God to help me put it together.

A couple of years ago, I had a patient who had served on active duty with the US Army Rangers in combat. At the time of his treatment, he was in civilian life and had a severe alcohol problem. I knew he was generally a very angry man. He didn't think much of our treatment program or our staff, and he completely disrespected the peer group as a bunch of whiners. I had him in for a spiritual-care consult to talk about God and the first three steps of A.A.

In the course of the consult, I mentioned that he used to be a US Army Ranger. He corrected me: "I *am* a Ranger. Once a Ranger, always a Ranger." I observed that I had heard that the Rangers always carried out their dead, never leaving a fellow Ranger behind on the field of battle. He said that was true and was a point of pride for them. I started a sentence by saying I was never in the military, and he interrupted me: "And it shows!" I slipped in a question about whether he volunteered for the Rangers, and he looked at me as if I were stupid and pointed out that the whole Army is a volunteer one. We had a discussion about all the things one must do to become a Ranger, the intensity of the training, the dedication and endurance it takes to become one. I affirmed him for his achievements and his service, while asking God for help in reaching him.

Then I turned on him. I pointed a finger at his face and barked: "*You* volunteered for treatment on Silkworth unit. The Silkworth peers are your unit. If you are willing to leave one Silkworth brother behind to *die* of this disease, then you're not a *real* Ranger any more!"

I thought he was about to rip my head off. He turned purple. Veins stood out on his neck. He got up and walked out, much to my relief. He went back to the Silkworth unit and organized his peers. By the end of the week, they were making their beds so that a quarter would bounce off them. "Line up for lecture" meant "LINE UP FOR LECTURE!" He became the peer leader.

I had trusted God for some insight, and this time I was able to reach the patient. I also trust God when we can't reach someone. I trust that God will go with our patient who isn't getting sober this time and give that alcoholic or addict another chance. We are not God. Only God is God.

SERVICE

To be sober, we serve others. God gave us the gift of recovery, but we are given it for a purpose: we are here on earth to serve others. In the last chapter of this book, I will write about the promises of recovery and the happiness that comes with sobriety. The happiness becomes real.

The spiritual principle of Step Twelve is service. There is no evidence that an eleven-and-a-half-step program really works: "Having had a spiritual awakening as the result of these steps—I'm outta here, good luck to you!" Service doesn't just complete our program, it makes it possible. Our recovery is subject to entropy, the force in the universe that tends to make everything lose its energy, wind down, and become lukewarm. Service gives our recovery new energy and new strength.

When I was drinking and drugging, I focused on getting, not giving. I had a greedy heart. The only place I was generous was in my relationship with the liquor industry. I never resented giving them money. My relationships with others were based on my constant desire to get them to do what I wanted.

When I got sober, selfishness and self-centeredness did not just automatically fade away. The idea that I should actually be of service to my wife came slowly. I got a major clue one day at a car dealership. I was the pastor of a church in northern New Hampshire, and the car dealer sold Volvos and Chevrolets. I was in the service department to pick up my new Volvo from its six-hundred-mile checkup.

A parishioner of mine was there with his new Chevy, and he was furious, for a good reason. The exhaust system was falling off his new car, and they wouldn't do anything about it. The rationale was that Chevy wasn't yet manufacturing spare parts because it was a brand-new model and none of them were supposed to fail yet. Also, the dealership wouldn't weld it together for free because Chevrolet wouldn't pay them to weld it under warranty—only parts replacements were covered under the warranty, not welding. They wouldn't do anything. He was shut out. He raged at them for a while, and they still did nothing. He left furious, his exhaust system held together with duct tape and clamps.

I stayed out of it. When they gave me my car, they said they had replaced both side mirrors under warranty. I hadn't known there was anything wrong with them. They cited some little brown spots on the mirrors. I commented on how my experience was totally different from the man with the Chevy, adding that it must be based on what the manufacturer is willing to pay for. The service manager said it was totally different, that Volvo was really strict with them. I asked what he meant. He said, "Volvo's standard is that fixing the car is not enough. We have to fix the car and serve the customer in such a way, that the service visit confirms in the customer's mind that they made the right choice when they bought a Volvo."

I thought, *I could use that at home.* Instead of banging in the door and saying, "What's to eat...wanna have sex?" as I did when drinking, I could adopt this standard: when I come home, the way I greet my wife in the first fifteen minutes should confirm in her mind that she made the right decision when she decided to marry me (and it's no fair if the second fifteen minutes go downhill).

The traditions of the Twelve Step programs say our leaders are but trusted servants—they do not govern. If we have ever tried to govern our spouses, we have rapidly seen what a bad idea that is. If we try serving our spouses, trying to see that their lives are good in every way, we will discover the benefits of service right in our homes.

The right service changes us, right away. These days, the thing that challenges my sobriety the most is loneliness. When my wife goes away, I'm OK for seven to ten days. Around two weeks, I start to get lonely. She's got a full life of her own, and now that she's retired, she travels more. This winter she's visiting friends in Florida and then going to Bolivia with a nonprofit group to open a new medical clinic in a poor community way up in the mountains. She'll be away for a few weeks. I might get lonely and restless.

I already know the fastest cure for that restlessness. My Monday night meeting makes a service commitment to the Saint Paul, Minnesota, detox center. When I go there, I always feel better. I can't identify exactly why, but it works every time.

I think of my speaking engagements and my writing as a form of service. I started writing essays for Hazelden newsletters. I put my lectures on iTunes, CDBaby.com, and Amazon.com to make them available. I have ideas on recovery, and I try to get them out in the hope of being of service to someone. Sometimes I get e-mails at Hazelden from people who found the ideas to be useful, and it feels good.

Frederick Buechner, in his book *Wishful Thinking*, wrote: "The more you get, the more you have. The more you give away in love and service, the more you *are*."

KEEP COMING BACK

To be sober, we keep coming back to our Twelve Step fellowships. I actually started going to meetings thirty-seven years ago, thirteen years before I got sober.

I started going to meetings when I was teaching a graduate course on addictions. I fell into teaching either by accident or by God's plan (it's hard to tell the difference sometimes). I had been teaching a class on interventions because, as a pastor, I did a very large number of interventions in my community. Then the addictions-course instructor had a heart attack two weeks before the start of classes, and I was asked to take over that course. I did so as a favor to the department chair. I was reading the text a week ahead of the students and relying on guest lecturers like myself. I decided that if I wanted to understand alcoholism, I should go where the alcoholics were, so I started attending open A.A. meetings.

I walked in and was amazed. I felt immediately at home. These were my people! Where had they been all my life? I instinctively understood them, and they seemed to all know me as if they were my long-lost brothers and sisters.

I felt really sad that I wasn't an alcoholic. If only I was an alcoholic, I thought, then I would qualify for membership. I kept going to open meetings, respecting the third tradition, in order to learn, but also because it felt good. I went to open meetings for thirteen years as I moved from one community to another.

Everyone else would introduce themselves and say, "And I'm an alcoholic." I would say, "Hi, I'm John, and I'm happy to be here." They were open meetings, so no one challenged me. Occasionally, I'd overhear someone saying in the background, "He almost admitted it," but I was truly clueless.

They weren't wasted years. I came to love the program. By the time I figured out that I was an alcoholic, there was no question about where to go and what to do. After thirteen years of attending open meetings while drinking and remaining clueless about myself, I finally "joined" the program.

After thirty-seven years of meetings, one might think that the chances of hearing something really new are small, but I keep getting new insights. Not long ago a man said, "No matter how far down the road of alcoholism I get, I'm always the same distance from the ditch." I like that. It's a good reminder for me at twenty-four years sober.

I also go because it is one of the three places in life where I find true love and acceptance; the others are with God and my wife and daughters. Our fellowship is wonderfully tolerant of our eccentricity, our defects, and even our relapses and failures. They just look at us and say, "Keep coming back—it works!"

Being in the fellowship also gives us the opportunity to take up recovery as our own cause. Some people have a political party or a sports team as their cause. They get all excited for a championship or an election. They volunteer for a campaign or pay top dollar for Super Bowl tickets so they can cheer for their team's victory.

We can make our fellow alcoholics and addicts our cause. A.A. says its primary purpose is for its members to stay sober and help other alcoholics achieve sobriety. NA says its primary purpose is that no addict seeking recovery need die. We develop a great enthusiasm when we adopt all the alcoholics and all the addicts as our cause.

If we pull apart the word *enthusiasm* into its pieces, it comes apart as *en-thusia-ism*. "En" means "in"; "thusia" is from the ancient Greek word "theos," or "God"; and "ism" is a system of belief, like communism or capitalism.

So "enthusiasm" is a belief system based on allowing the spirit of God to fill us with…enthusiasm! As we start to feel great, we naturally want this for all the alcoholics and all the addicts who still suffer.

A patient once asked me, "How do you know when you've really had a spiritual awakening?" I thought a minute about what was blocking him, then said, "When you truly love all the alcoholics and all the addicts, including the unpleasant ones who are still drinking and drugging, then you will have had your spiritual awakening." If we keep coming back, that love will grow and we will continue to wake up.

PRAYER AND MEDITATION

To be sober, we pray, which is speaking to God. We also meditate, which is listening to God, so that we may know and do God's will. We can pray any way we want to. A spiritual friend once said to me, "If we get into prayer, all of life can be a prayer." At the time I thought he was just being mystical, but I've come to think it is possible to live more and more of our waking minutes in conscious contact with God, or awareness of being in the presence of God.

We start by just talking to God. We talk out loud if we like, we talk inside our heads if the situation warrants. I have not gotten very much out of formal written prayers in terms of communicating with God. I find them better for communicating with myself. The Serenity Prayer hasn't put me in touch with God, but it has helped me calm myself. The prayers associated with the various steps in the A.A. Big Book haven't put me in touch with God when I have prayed them, but they have been important sources of insight for me on how to work those steps. For other people, they have been vital connections to God. We are all different.

My prayers have been very direct and personal. They haven't always worked, in the sense of getting results. When I was a young child, my mother taught me the little children's prayer:

> *Now I lay me down to sleep,*
> *I pray the Lord my soul to keep.*
> *If I die before I wake,*
> *I pray the Lord my soul to take.*

Then, after I was asleep, her drinking would make her angry, and she would sometimes come into my bedroom and beat me. I would awaken to her fury. If the beating went on for some time, I would become afraid of dying. I would ask God to let me die and go live with him, just like the prayer said, because it hurt so bad to live there and be beaten. Then she would stop beating me and go away. I didn't die, and the violence didn't stop. I felt abandoned by my parents and abandoned by God. As far as I could tell, my prayers didn't work.

I didn't pray again until after God broke into my life, about age twenty, with the absurd idea that I was meant to become a minister. I started a conversation in my head with, "You've got to be kidding," and thereafter it was mostly a monologue on my part.

When we pray, we end up with some mental image of the God to whom we are praying, if only because it is difficult to imagine a blank space. My mental image of God is pretty close to the portrayal of God in the 1980s movie *Oh God!* with George Burns and John Denver. George Burns portrayed God as a comedic Jewish taxi driver. That's my mental picture of God, a supreme being with a strong sense of irony. One of my jokes is that God gave his "Chosen People" the only Middle Eastern country with no oil.

If that's my mental image, that leaves me in the role played by John Denver, a guy with a lot of questions and complaints for God. Oddly enough, I trust God enough to ask questions and make complaints.

Back when I was still drinking but going to meetings and trying to sort out my life, I went to a psychiatrist to try to work out all the trauma and confusion in my mind. We had unpacked some of the abuse stories. At that point, he noticed my almost total lack of emotions. He wanted me to find my anger. I had none. He was encouraging me to find my anger over the abuse, and I just couldn't get in touch with it. In retrospect, perhaps I was protecting him from being in the room when I found it.

I found my anger all at once while I was driving on an expressway, not near an exit. I was in the center lane going seventy miles an hour, and I found it all—and there was a lot. It was as if the roof of the car was peeled off and a garbage truck dumped its whole load into the car at once. I was totally filled with rage.

I could tell that the freeway was not a good place to express all that rage, but I wasn't near an exit. I grabbed the steering wheel hard with both hands and tried to break it. It felt like physical rage. Then I yelled, "ANGRY! ANGRY! ANGRY!" over and over as loud as I could until my throat hurt. I was yelling at God because God is always right there and my rage was cosmic-sized. It felt as if my rage filled the whole universe. I was still driving, now in the slow lane, safely, looking for the exit.

I finally got off the expressway and stopped, thoroughly shaken. Then a little voice in my head, which sounded like God, said, "John, you can get well, or you can get even. Pick one."

"NO! I want them both. I want to get well, and I want to get even!" There was no further word in my head. I knew the message was from God, and I knew it was true. I could get well, or I could get even, but I couldn't get both.

I wanted revenge so badly. I decided not to decide, but I knew what the ultimate decision would be. I just didn't want to make it. Within a couple of days, I had chosen to get well and let go of revenge. I went to the therapist and told him all that had happened in a week.

Now that I am praying for the right motives and returning to God when I face indecision, my friend's suggestion that all of life can be a prayer is closer to becoming true. We can live more of our hours in conscious contact with God. This just means that we are aware God exists and we benefit from thinking about God's will for our lives.

Whatever allows us to feel closer to God and to be closer to God is a good prayer. I have not been a Catholic since I was eight years old, but I still have a sentimental tie to Saint Patrick's Cathedral in New York City. New York is my home, and when in Manhattan I often stop in, light a candle, and say a prayer for my mother, who has been dead now for years.

Why? I don't know, but it feels right. She was a Catholic all her life. She hated the church, but only because her life was dominated by addiction and hatred. She was never healed or cured in this life, and only God has the power to touch her or have mercy on her. So I light a candle.

The bottom line is, we pray any way we want to. But when we are done praying, we meditate, too. After we talk, we listen, because we need to know what God has to say to us.

The Twelve Step programs also have a remarkable reversal in how they teach us to pray. Most prayer, including most church prayer, is essentially more magical than faithful. That is, we are trying to say the right words to get God to do our will. The Twelve Step programs tell us to pray to get us to do God's will. This is the opposite of "normal" prayer. In magic, we try to find the magic words to get God to do what we want. In faith, we try to line ourselves up to do what God wants. They are different.

Alcoholics and addicts have plenty of experience with magical prayers that don't work. "Lord, if you get me out of this mess, I promise never to drink or use again." We might get out of that mess, but our promise is empty. Step Eleven asks us to pray only for knowledge of God's will for our lives and for the power to carry that out. As we go through our days, we keep an open mind on the question of what God wants us to do about the next thing that happens.

For example, consider the question of my "starter marriage" to Kathy. We married when I graduated from college and she was still in school. We were married for three and a half years, and then she left me, saying I was "boring." I was, I thought, devastated. I couldn't imagine that she would ever leave me. I didn't see it coming and was shocked and dismayed. I gave her most of the assets and kept the debt. I gave her the new car and kept the junker. She even took my pet cat, which I had found as a stray.

Looking back, the truth is that I actually *was* boring. All I did in the evening was drink. I'd go to work and school, come home and drink. I didn't want to do anything but drink. I was boring, and she left.

Thirty-eight years later, when I was long sober and married to Priscilla, I got a group e-mail that Kathy sent to all her friends. It was a terrible story. She had developed advanced cancer and was no longer able to work. She was running out of money and was living in a metal camping trailer in a campground in New Jersey. My first thought was that the news was terrible and I should say a prayer for her. Then I thought, *Big deal. Saying a prayer for her takes ten seconds. Then I can forget about her and move on.* I remembered Step Eleven and praying for knowledge of God's will for *my* life, not hers. I decided to keep an open mind on the subject of what God wanted me to do.

The thought came to me that I should visit her. I didn't know if she wanted a visit, so I called her. She said she would welcome a visit, so I set one up. She lived nine hundred miles from me. As we talked on the phone, I found out she had been approved for government disability payments, but there was a five-month gap with no payments before a cash flow would begin. So I talked to Priscilla, and we agreed to offer Kathy the equivalent of those five months of payments that the government wasn't making so she could get out of the camping trailer and into an apartment before winter. I made my visit, and we ended up helping Kathy during the last eighteen months of her life before she died of her cancer.

I believe my response was better than just saying a prayer that God would do something good. The truth is that I did love Kathy, and I did make a commitment to her once, and I could help her. Without Step Eleven, it would never have occurred to me to do it. We pray and meditate to help us know and do God's will.

GRATITUDE

To stay sober, we remember the past, and we cultivate gratitude in our hearts for the gift of recovery. If resentments are a symptom of the disease of addiction, then gratitude is both the most reliable symptom and the most accurate sign of recovery. Gratitude is a symptom of recovery because we can feel it in our hearts, and it is a sign of recovery because others can see it in our speech, actions, and attitude.

If our recovery were an achievement, we could be proud of it because it would belong to us; it would be ours. However, our recovery is a gift from a Higher Power; therefore, we are grateful instead of proud; and it is a treasure to be shared with the whole recovery community.

I remember my past. I started on drugs and alcohol together to treat the pain of child abuse and torture. I continued to drink and drug to blot out the consciousness of my intolerable situations, both the one I came from and the one I was creating through my alcohol and drug use.

I am not grateful for every element of my life and every event in my history. I can see value in every experience, but some of the experiences were just evil. I am not grateful for evil. I am grateful to have survived the bad things. I am not one to make everything good or to find a good purpose in everything, but I believe life is fundamentally good and am willing to join in a common purpose with anyone who is working to make life better. I am grateful for every good effort, goodwill, good intention, and good action I have encountered along the way.

WE CAN STAY SOBER

The grace and power of God, the Twelve Step fellowships, my sober friends and allies, and the principles of these programs have made recovery possible, reliable, and ultimately a source of joy and happiness. My first sponsor promised me that if I read chapters 5 and 6 of the Big Book and did what they said, I would never drink or use again. The gift of recovery started there for me, but the program and the process of recovery has gone on to provide everything I've ever wanted in life, and the rest of this book is about how that can happen for all of us. Staying sober is the admission ticket to a way of life that is ultimately happier than any other way.

I learned to start my day with the First Step of A.A. I admit that I am powerless over alcohol and that my life had become unmanageable. My life never has to be unmanageable again as long as I rely on God, my program, and my sober friends.

CHAPTER 2:

SPIRITUALITY AND RECOVERY

———

Many people say "I'm not religious, I'm spiritual", but when asked what they mean by "spiritual" they have no idea beyond "not religious". Addiction is powerful, We need a spirituality that is powerful enough to beat our addictions every day. We need a team, consisting of a higher power that is real, sober friends who are real, and our own real, sober, and alert selves.

WHY SPIRITUALITY?

To understand the role of spirituality in recovery, it helps to understand the disease from which we are recovering. I like the definition that Craig Nakken uses in his book *The Addictive Personality*. He calls addiction "a pathological relationship of love and trust with an object or an event." Pathological means "disease causing." Addiction is a disease-causing relationship. Alcohol is an object. Heroin is an object. Compulsive gambling is an event. Our relationship with alcohol, heroin, or gambling is making us sick. Even though I don't drink or drug today, I still have a pathological relationship with alcohol, benzodiazepines, and opiates, in that if I ingest any of them, all of my addiction, and more, will come roaring back. Therefore, I am still an alcoholic and an addict.

What does that have to do with spirituality? The only method of treating alcoholism and drug addiction that has resulted in large numbers of clean and sober people over a long period of time has been Alcoholics Anonymous and Narcotics Anonymous. In most American communities, there is one Twelve Step meeting for every thousand people. No other group, model, or program has even one-tenth the success rate of A.A. and N.A. Some short-term research studies do show short-term success with other models, but when you explore your own community, looking for people with long-term sobriety who are using another model, it is extremely difficult to find anyone.

Alcoholics Anonymous has "three pertinent ideas" in the chapter "How it Works":

- (a) That we were alcoholic and could not manage our own lives.
- (b) That probably no human power could have relieved our alcoholism
- (c) That God could and would if He were sought.

The book doesn't say, "if God were found"; it says, "if God were sought." This is because we are not, ultimately, going to "find" God. I try to use logic whenever I can. If there is a God, and if this God can help me and every other alcoholic and addict wherever and whenever we need help with recovery, then the chances that I will fully understand this God are very close to zero. I can seek God, I can have a relationship with God, I can experience God, but I cannot define, understand, predict, or control God. If I grasp this, then I can finally, as A.A. says, "let go and let God."

A.A. discovered early in its development that some form of spiritual awakening was needed for recovery, but it also discovered that religious controversy, or even preaching a Christian gospel, was nothing but trouble. Bill Wilson, after his spiritual awakening, went out preaching to drunks. None of them got sober. The group that later became Alcoholics Anonymous broke away from the Oxford Group because the Oxford Group was affiliated with Protestant churches. In the 1930s Protestants and Catholics did not associate together in groups. The alcoholics separated from the Oxford Group, in part, because they didn't want to deny Catholics the opportunity to recover with them. In treatment centers and in A.A. and N.A. today, members have to reassure newcomers that the program is spiritual, not religious.

It took me a long time to figure out I was an alcoholic and could not manage my own life. This was because my extreme unmanageability happened in my twenties, and I managed to reduce my intake and achieve some level of manageability in my thirties. I had the outer structure of manageability: a home, a wife, a job, a car, and an address. I was treating life as if it were a scavenger hunt. I had found all the pieces and put them together, so I concluded that I must be OK. It was only when I met the alcoholic men at Hazelden that I realized I was one of them.

By the time I realized I was an alcoholic, I knew that no human power could relieve my alcoholism. Once I got the whiskey, Valium, and Percodan out of my brain, I could recall that I had already tried to quit many times and failed. I knew there was much more to the A.A. program than Phil and Joe and my A.A. friends. I believed them when they said that God could and would relieve my addiction if he were sought.

I already believed in God but only felt God's presence once in a while. It's really hard to feel God's presence when you're drunk. Sometimes I felt God when I was preaching really well in church. Sometimes I felt God when visiting people in the hospital. I felt God most frequently when conducting the sacrament of the Lord's Supper, which is the Methodist equivalent of the Catholic Mass. The Methodist Church uses grape juice, not wine, out of a historic concern for alcoholics that goes back to the 1700s. I never noticed the irony of needing a drink or some Valium to steady me for an alcohol-free sacrament, but I still felt God's presence during it. No matter what fog I was in, when I would say to people, "The body of Christ, broken for you" and "The blood of Christ, shed for you," it was all real.

Most of the time, the unholy trinity—whiskey, Valium, and Percodan—cut me off from God, other people, and myself.

WHAT IS SPIRITUALITY?

There are many definitions of spirituality. I define spirituality as the quality or nature of our relationships in three dimensions: relationships with our Higher Power, with ourselves, and with other people. As such, everyone has some spirituality. It might be terrible, but we've all got some. Our spirituality is the theme that runs through all three relationships. It unites us, animates us, and makes us who we are.

It is easier to see this theme in others, because we look at other people a lot more than we look at ourselves. Try thinking of a variety of people you know. Then fill in the blank in this sentence: "He/she has a spirit of _____." Whatever word you put in the blank defines that person's spirit. If someone has a spirit of greed, they will be greedy everywhere they go, and conflicts in their lives will be resolved in favor of whatever gets them more money; they will complain to God, or to the universe, about not having enough money. If they have a spirit of provocation, they will provoke arguments everywhere they go; they will resent God for not running the universe well. If they have a spirit of despair, they will be downhearted about most things and won't want to take on new projects or new relationships because they have learned that most things fail; they will expect nothing from God, either. If they have a spirit of cheerfulness, they will spread cheer to others and will expect that God is good. If they have a spirit of industriousness, they will be willing workers and see God as a partner.

The three relationships—with Higher Power, self, and others—are closely intertwined. They can't be effectively separated. I don't think it is possible to love God, be at peace with yourself, and treat everyone else like dirt. It just doesn't happen. Any improvement in one of the three relationships lifts the other two. Any breakdown in one of the three relationships tears the other two down. If you have an ugly fight with the person you love, you aren't likely to go to bed and say your prayers to God, because you are embarrassed about your conduct. Also, you won't feel very good about yourself. So all three relationships—Higher Power, self, and others—are damaged, even though you are only fighting with one person.

If you want to improve your spirituality right away, try treating every human being you meet as if he or she were a beloved child of a Higher Power. That doesn't mean you have to love everyone right away. In some cases, that might be too much of a stretch to make. At least imagine that they have a Higher Power and that their Higher Power loves them. Once you imagine all people as beloved children of their Higher Power, you will start treating them with dignity and respect. Your relationship with them will improve because you are treating them better. You will feel better about yourself because your conduct is better. It will gradually dawn on you that if everyone else has a loving Higher Power, so do you, and your whole attitude and outlook on life will improve. You will lighten up.

Our spiritual state has more to do with our future than anything else does. The A.A.'s Big Book states:

Selfishness—self-centeredness! That, we think, is the root of our troubles. Driven by a hundred forms of fear, self-delusion, self-seeking, and self-pity, we step on the toes of our fellows and they retaliate…

So our troubles, we think, are basically of our own making. They arise out of ourselves, and the alcoholic is an extreme example of self-will run riot, though he usually doesn't think so. Above everything, we alcoholics must be rid of this selfishness. We must, or it kills us! God makes this possible. (p. 62)

In the previous chapter, "Staying Sober," I wrote about needing to make the daily decision to put our sobriety first. That is accompanied by daily attention to our spiritual condition. A key question is whether our spiritual condition is balanced or unbalanced. Are we thinking only of ourselves, or are we thinking of the quality of our relationships with our Higher Power, ourselves, and other people?

Selfishness as a spiritual state isn't always unattractive and doesn't always bring negative consequences. The standard American success story can still be predominantly selfish. The model of the "self-made man" still garners respect and admiration if that self-made person appears to be "making it" in America. As we lose interest in selfish things and gain interest in our spirituality, we discover a whole new source of joy and happiness. I've seen two versions of this bumper sticker: "He who dies with the most toys, wins," and "He who dies with the most toys—dies." Peter Lynch, one of America's most successful investors, once said, "No one ever said on his deathbed, 'Gee, I wish I had spent more time at the office.'"

In the Big Book's text on Step Ten, in which we continue to take personal inventory, the book says we have entered the world of the spirit, that we have ceased fighting anything or anyone—even alcohol—and that love and tolerance of others is our code. How I read that is that I love what is loveable and tolerate whatever I cannot manage to love. I am leaving behind the old way of life, when I believed that every day it was "me against the world." Increasingly, I am able to receive the world just the way it actually is, on the basis of love and tolerance. It's not all the time—but that's a sign I continue to need God's help. At least I know where I have come from, and I know where I am going.

WHAT IS RELIGION?

Religions are systems of beliefs and behaviors that are intended to bring people into a closer relationship with God as those religions understand God. Religious doctrines are often well-organized sets of beliefs. Religious rituals are often well-organized behaviors. Both are intended to lead us to know, understand, and celebrate the truth about God, Higher Power, or Ultimate Truth, as it is taught in that religion. The main idea is that if we know what the truth is, then we will act on that truth, and the truth will help us live a better life and bring us into a better relationship with the central focus of that religion.

The first problem that shows up with religion and alcoholism is that people focus on beliefs instead of behaviors, and then show bad behaviors while disagreeing about beliefs. There are a great number of religions, many of which disagree about the nature of God and even disagree about whether there is a God. For example, the *Handbook of American Denominations* lists more than sixteen hundred denominations. All religions come to us with a claim of truth—which tends to be a set of facts—that one is meant to accept. Acceptance of this body of doctrine is supposed to give us a spiritual benefit: wisdom, serenity, forgiveness, or even eternal life. My experience suggests that simply accepting doctrines as true does not, by itself, change us. We need to change not just our beliefs about God but also our relationship with God. An angry nonbeliever who starts to believe may become an angry believer. If we claim that our relationship with God has changed but our relationships with other people and with ourselves are unchanged, it is questionable whether our relationship with God has changed at all.

The second problem that shows up with religion and alcoholism is that some religions regard drinking or drunkenness as sinful. This can lead to attempts to treat alcoholism and addiction with condemnation and punishment or with confession. Confession works for sin but not for disease. One might as well ask diabetics to confess their diabetes.

An important distinction between spirituality and religion is that spirituality is based on our relationship with a Higher Power and our experience of that Higher Power being active in our lives, as well as the stories of other alcoholics and addicts. Religion is based on a set of beliefs in a Higher Power that have come from history, instruction, and revealed literature.

I learned the Christian religion in Sunday school, in church, and in individual Bible readings. Later, I learned the religion in two graduate schools of theology, including Bible study in the original languages of the Bible. I learned the practical application of the Christian faith in eighteen years as a parish pastor. My estimate is that I got from those endeavors about a quarter of the spirituality I have today. The other three-quarters I picked up along the way in Twelve Step programs.

My experiences of God were confusing and disappointing when I was young. As I described in chapter 1, my mom had taught me the little kid's prayer:

Now I lay me down to sleep,
I pray the Lord my soul to keep.
If I die before I wake,
I pray the Lord my soul to take.

And then, once asleep, I would be awakened by a beating. If the beating went on for a long time, I would pray to God to let me die. He didn't. I felt abandoned by my parents and abandoned by God. I still believed in God, but I believed he wouldn't help me.

In sixth grade, I "ran away" twenty blocks to the home of my church's youth minister. I told him all about the abuse. He listened patiently, using what I now recognize as the skills of reflective listening. He told me to wait, and he left the room. He then called my parents, told them everything I had said, and sent me home, only to be beaten again for "telling." That convinced me that God would not do anything for me.

I still believed in God. I still had Christian beliefs. But I had the spirituality of a rock. "I feel nothing. I am not hungry. I am not cold. I love no one. I need nothing."

Years later, improbably, I was seized with the certainty that God wanted me to become a minister. I was a highly unlikely prospect. I was on the brink of flunking out of college due to failing every course. I was failing every course due to drinking so much that I didn't know what classes I was flunking. I immediately misinterpreted my new insight to mean that God would keep me from flunking out. I promptly flunked out.

However, I got back in—and flunked out again. Then I got back in and had an undistinguished academic career at Rutgers. Somehow, Princeton Theological Seminary took me. I flunked theology my first year, drank my way through school, and finished a year late, but I finished. I have a large diploma from Princeton on my office wall. It's all in Latin. I have a diploma I can't read from a school I can't remember, but I've got a prestigious theological education.

My relationship with God continued as God sent lots of homeless alcoholics to my door as a pastor. I made it my business to find out what I could do for them. My efforts led to my interest in treatment and recovery, all while I was unaware of my own need for recovery and sobriety. My work with people in pain gave me the spiritual gifts of discernment and compassion, so I became less of a rock.

I remember one day when I was doing hospital calling on sick people. In the hallway I saw a woman who attended my church and who worked in the hospital. She saw me, said, "Oh, good! I need a hug!" and came toward me. I was still a rock who did not hug people. I thought, *Oh no! How do I get out of this?* I decided to fake a hug because I couldn't think of a reason to reject her. So I pretended I was a mime, silently acting out a hug. She didn't notice it was a fake. She said, "Thanks! I needed that!" and went away happy. I was surprised to feel a feeling. I kind of liked it. I was starting to discover some spirituality, the spirituality of loving relationships, to go alongside my correct Christian beliefs.

After attending A.A. for a few months, I was amazed to discover that God was more real to me in the church basement with the A.A. people than in the church sanctuary upstairs. On Sunday mornings, I talked about God and people listened. Then, at the door, they would give me feedback about how well or poorly I had talked about God, but for the most part, they did not talk about how God was active in their lives. Here, in the basement, people did—all the time.

THE RELATIONSHIP BETWEEN RELIGION AND SPIRITUALITY

Now I have both a religion and positive spirituality. Religion and spirituality are different, not opposite. We can have both, and they complement each other. One of the most negative things I hear at Twelve Step meetings is this: "Religion is for people who are afraid of hell, and the program is for people who have already been there." I don't like that saying for a number of reasons: it is condescending to religious people; it isn't true that all religious people are afraid of hell; and not all recovering people have been through hell—many have stopped in time to avoid serious consequences. The statement sets up a phony conflict between religion and the recovery program.

At the other extreme, there are religious people who don't approve of Twelve Step programs because they think the programs are incompatible with their religion. I sometimes meet with "born-again Christians" who are concerned that A.A. doesn't teach "in the name of Jesus." I point out that Christianity is, in effect, treatment for sin. In Christianity, the problem is sin and the solution is salvation. A.A. is treatment for alcoholism. The problem is that we are powerless over alcohol, and the solution is to get power from a Higher Power in a spiritual program with twelve steps. So, Christian alcoholics can go to church and confess their sins to obtain forgiveness of sins, and they can go to A.A. to successfully manage their alcoholism. The point is to pick the right tool for the job. Going to church won't keep me sober, and A.A. never claimed to forgive my sins.

A SUGGESTED MINIMUM STANDARD FOR A HIGHER POWER

How "high" does a Higher Power need to be? Remembering that I am powerless over alcohol and over addiction, my Higher Power needs to be more powerful than the addiction to alcohol, or it will be useless. My minimum standard for a Higher Power has three parts: (1) it is not me, (2) it is more powerful than me, and (3) it wants to help me.

1. I cannot be my own Higher Power. Many of us have tried, without success. This is not a "self-help program."

Self-help is a fantasy. It's a lot like tickling yourself. It seems, conceptually, like it ought to work—until you try. Nothing happens. You cannot tickle yourself. You can only be tickled in a relationship. I think this is because our brains are wired to ignore input from ourselves. This is convenient, because otherwise every time we rolled over in our sleep, we'd wake ourselves up. For example, sometimes I feel like drinking. Then I call an A.A. friend, and he says, "Well, don't drink," and I feel better. I could say it to myself, but if I say it to myself, I don't feel better. Another alcoholic has to say it for me to feel better. Only another alcoholic can be the voice of my Higher Power.

2. It has to be more powerful than me. I get tired. My A.A. friends never all get tired at the same time. I make mistakes. Somebody in A.A. has already made every mistake I can think up, so if I use them as consultants, I can stay out of a lot of trouble. I get weak. There's strength in numbers. I cannot inspire myself. God can inspire me.

3. A.A. and God want to help me. A.A. has taught me that when I turn my will and my life over to God, what I find there is care. That is the experience of a couple of million men and women who have gone before me, and it is reliable. I'm not going to find judgment or rejection, but care.

We can find these three things on three levels. The first level is our immediate peer group in treatment or in a Twelve Step program. The group isn't us, it is more powerful than us, and it wants to help us. The second level is the program as a whole. We can go to a different group, even in a different city, and gain access to the same power. The third level is our intangible but real Higher Power. Ultimately, we realize that on all three levels, "God is doing for us what we could not do for ourselves" (Big Book, p. 83).

HOW CAN WE BUILD OUR SPIRITUALITY?

We can build our spirituality in four ways: (1) do prayer and meditation; (2) surrender to God and trust in God, (3) take the Twelve Steps, and (4) practice the spiritual principles of the Twelve Steps. We do all these things in a fellowship with fellow alcoholics. They don't work well when we try to do them alone.

There are many long essays on prayer and meditation. This is a short one. Pray any way you want to. Pray out loud, pray silently. Pray by writing, pray by speaking, pray in the form of art work, pray in the form of working for others. Pray by praising, pray by complaining. Pray by repetition, pray by reading from great prayers of history, pray in silence and emptiness—but pray.

Meditation is listening. How would any other conversation go if you only spoke and then walked away without listening? Give God a chance to speak to you. Listen for the voice of inspiration. Listen for the voice of conscience. Listen for a word of comfort, of hope, of challenge. Listen for a response that isn't in words. Once I felt a sense like that of a child being tucked in at night by a loving parent.

Twelve Step programs suggest a big change in the way we usually pray. The change is so huge that it's easy to miss.

Most of our prayers, including most of our church prayers, are more magical than faithful.

In magic, we try to say the magic words to get God to do our will. In faith, we try to align ourselves with God's will. The two are exactly opposite. Step Eleven calls for faith when it talks about "praying only for knowledge of God's will for our lives and the power to carry that out" (Big Book, p. 60).

We have been praying for God to know *our* will for *God's* life, and now we start praying to know *God's* will for *our* life and to actually be granted the power to do it. This makes life different.

Prayer is much more than a wish list. The wish list is for Santa Claus. I never really believed in him. Prayer and meditation connect us with God, and when we are communicating freely and opening our hearts to receive what our Higher Power has for us, our spirituality grows.

I will cover the other three ways to build spirituality—surrender and trust, take the Twelve Steps, and practice the spiritual principles of the Twelve Steps—in the next two chapters of this book.

By this point in the book, we can recognize the importance of spirituality in our recovery, identify key elements of our own spirituality, decide if there is a productive place in our lives for a religion or religious heritage, begin to identify our Higher Power, and begin to pray and meditate. Those things add up to spiritual progress.

CHAPTER 3:

SURRENDER AND TRUST

For a recovery that can bring us all the way into happiness, we need to surrender to a Higher Power and trust in that Higher Power. The key to moving forward toward surrender and trust is accepting life on life's terms, just exactly the way it is right now.

WHAT IS SURRENDER?

During the opening of every A.A. meeting, alcoholics read to each other a passage from the Big Book chapter "How It Works." In that passage, we read:

> *Some of us have tried to hold on to our old ideas and the result was nil until we let go absolutely. (p. 58)*

Surrender is letting go absolutely: letting go of our old ideas, of the myth of self-sufficiency, of the notion that we can control the outcome of our own lives and the lives of others, and of the fatal concept that we can beat alcoholism and addiction on our own.

We alcoholics and addicts need to surrender, to let go absolutely of our resistance to recovery, but it is hard to do that. One of the reasons it is hard to surrender is the bad reputation of the word "surrender." We tend to associate "surrender" with "losing," and no one wants to be a "loser." Also, as alcoholics and addicts, our experience of addiction is one of losing control internally. As we lose control of our life and experiences, we try to balance it by becoming extremely controlling of everything outside of ourselves. Thus, anything that suggests giving up any control is extremely aversive. It makes us feel like we will disintegrate and fly apart. As our addictions grow, it takes more and more effort to control our usage or withdrawal, our access to our supply, and what other people know about us. We put ever more effort into controlling our drugs, other people, and life itself. Every new problem brings out the same response: more controlling behaviors. When we join a Twelve Step program and are confronted with a slogan like "Let go and let God," it seems completely crazy.

If we take another look at the word "surrender," we can find some potential there. What is its original context and meaning? We're in a war, the war is going very badly, and we're about to get killed. At the last minute, we tear up a white T-shirt, wave a piece of white cloth, and they don't kill us. This is not so bad. This has potential. This opens up new possibilities. We might escape from the enemy. Our side might win the war and liberate us. There is hope in our surrender.

Another meaning of the word "surrender" is to exchange one thing for another. We surrender something we are willing to part with in return for something we want more. When I was in junior high school, I rode a suburban bus on which the fare was set by zones. I told the driver where I wanted to go. He told me what the fare was. I gave him money. He gave me a receipt. The receipt listed the amount paid and the phrase "Surrender when leaving coach." That didn't mean I had to get off the bus with my arms raised; it meant I was trading in the fare I had paid in return for the ride. I was trading in the money, which I was willing to give up, in return for the ride, which is what I really wanted.

The Twelve Step programs invite us to trade in our old way of life in return for a new one, one that promises the care of a loving Higher Power and the fellowship of men and women who understand us and will support us. We are asked to trade in our powerlessness over alcohol and drugs in return for a Power greater than ourselves that will restore us to sanity.

In this program, I surrendered, or traded in, my skill at lying in return for the trust of my wife and children. I surrendered my sense of being alone and discovered both fellowship and solitude. Even as I surrender, or trade in, my pain, I find comfort. But it has been a slow process, because so much of what is natural in me resists letting go of anything.

Dr. Harry Tiebout, a psychiatrist who advised Bill Wilson and the founders of A.A., wrote about the difference between surrender and compliance in therapy. In compliance, we do what we are told. In surrender, we let go of all of our resistance to change and growth.

MOVING TOWARD SURRENDER

As I look at myself and other alcoholics and addicts, I see four stages that we move through: defiance, submission, compliance, and surrender.

At each stage of our movement toward surrender, there may be a difference between what our conscious minds think and what our unconscious minds think. We often experience conflict about our addictions, which is natural because our addictions are destroying us. The destruction of a human being is worth fighting over, so conflict is natural. Sometimes the conflict is within ourselves, and sometimes the conflict is between ourselves and other people. The chart below maps out the state of our conscious and unconscious minds at each stage of recovery, showing the changes as we move from defiance toward surrender to a recovery and ultimately to a Higher Power.

State of Mind	Conscious mind is saying to recovery:	Unconscious mind is saying to recovery:
Defiance	NO!	No
Submission	No, but	No
Compliance	Yes, but	No
Surrender	Yes	Yes

DEFIANCE

Defiance is the natural state of the actively using addict. In defiance, we do not have much conflict inside ourselves because our conscious and our unconscious minds are united: we are saying a firm "NO!" to recovery. Our conflict is not inside ourselves, it is outside—between us and everyone else who is trying to get us to cut down or stop our chemical use. Defiance feels uncomfortable, but all our discomfort is attributed to other people: if only they would leave us alone, we believe, we would be fine!

When we are in defiance, we are sure we do not need recovery because we are sure we are not sick. We may be aware that we drink a lot, but we have an alibi system to explain away any evidence that we have a problem. We may say that everyone we know drinks like this or that there is a lot of drinking in our job, our neighborhood, our income level, our ethnic group, our friends, our relatives, our lifestyle. We seek out people who drink more than we do so that our drinking looks moderate. Above all, when we are in our defiance, we are never wrong, not about anything, ever.

When we are in defiance, we are the center of the universe. Absolutely everything and everyone is in orbit around us. Our thoughts, feelings, needs, wants, and plans are all that matter. We arrange everyone where we want them to be in our lives, maneuvering them by positive and negative reinforcement into playing the roles we have assigned to them: the spouse, the children, the attorney, the doctor, the counselor, the "friends," the drinking buddies, and so on. They, in turn, end up confused because our behavior does not make sense to them. They are missing the one bit of information that would allow them to make sense of our behavior: the fact that everything we say and do is carefully, if unconsciously, calculated to draw attention away from our alcoholism and addiction. We defy everyone, while surrendering to our addiction.

SUBMISSION

If other people catch on to our game and apply a lot of out-side pressure on us, we will grudgingly move from defiance to submission. In submission, our unconscious mind is still saying "No!" to recovery, but consciously we have moved from a firm "No!" to a "No, but…" Now we have inner conflict. We need to look like we are changing, without actually changing.

For example, we have just been arrested and lodged in an unfamiliar county jail. We have not yet learned that jail's drug-distribution system. We are involuntarily clean. We have no plans to remain clean, but we are clean and sober right now. We are submitting to abstinence.

Or, we get intervened on by our family and friends. They hire someone who seems to be the worst social worker in the world. They gather all our relatives and a few of our closest remaining friends, even the ones who drink more than we do, for a "surprise party." They all read these horrible letters that start off with "I'm here because I'm concerned about you…," and we just want to throw up. They have already bought a one-way airline ticket to Minnesota and packed all the wrong clothes in a suitcase, and now we find ourselves in treatment at Hazelden. There are no drinks in treatment. We are submitting to recovery. We are sober. We might have no plans to remain sober, but we are sober right now. This has potential, and we want to look like we are embracing that potential without actually doing it.

COMPLIANCE

In compliance, our conscious minds are saying a tentative "yes" to recovery, while our unconscious minds are still saying "no." This sets up a lot of internal conflict, and this internal conflict is part of the reason why we relapse. This is both the next phase of recovery and the most common state of recovering alcoholics and addicts. In compliance, the conscious mind says "I will recover" while the unconscious mind reserves the right to pick up and use chemicals again. The conscious mind makes a commitment to recovery, and the unconscious mind leaves loopholes in that commitment, to keep the option of relapse open.

I remember when I first got clean and sober from alcohol, Valium, and Percodan. I remember thinking that I was fully committed to sobriety, with ninety meetings in ninety days. At the time, I had also been an emergency medical technician on ambulances for many years, so I had already seen many of the things that could go wrong with people. I recall thinking: *I'm really committed to my sobriety, but if I had to have stomach surgery, not the little laparoscopic belly button kind, but the kind where they lay your stomach open like the hood of a car, and that kind really hurts, and the only kind of meds that really take care of that kind of pain are opiates, and they would probably trigger my drinking, but it wouldn't be my fault...*

I wasn't even sick, and yet I was planning that relapse! I had no stomach illness! No need for an operation! Why was I even thinking about this? I thought about it because I was "of two minds": the conscious mind that had made a commitment to sobriety and the unconscious mind that was searching for available loopholes to that commitment.

A common experience of compliance that alcoholics and nonalcoholics alike have is dieting. I have a long history of being overweight. I have even come to understand why I am overweight and the unconscious factors in it. Insight has brought about a forty-pound weight loss, but I am still overweight. The unconscious mind is a powerful driver. Many people have made a conscious decision to diet. As long as we comply with that diet, we will lose or stabilize normal weight. However, the conscious mind is thinking "diet," and the unconscious mind is thinking "cupcake," so as soon as our compliance slips, so does the diet. This is the source of "yo-yo dieting," in which our weight goes down and up and down and up again.

One of the ways Twelve Step programs work is simply their reinforcement of our conscious choices so our unconscious mind doesn't run our lives. This conscious reinforcement of our compliance has allowed people to use the Twelve Steps for many things, including food issues and gambling.

My first year of sobriety was built almost entirely on compliance. God was involved, but I needed all the power of God just to help me comply with the program an hour at a time for the first ninety days…and then four hours at a time, morning, afternoon, and evening…and then a day at a time. I can't remember when "God help me!" transitioned into "Let go and let God," but it gradually did.

Most recovering alcoholics and addicts are in compliance most of the time, and that's good enough to produce a sobriety that is satisfying. It just isn't great. I want to affirm compliance because it got me sober. In real life, we fluctuate between compliance and surrender. In theory, it should be possible to live in a state of surrender all the time. I just don't know anyone who has actually done it. On my good days, I fully surrender to God. On my bad days, when my spirituality is threadbare and I'm not really surrendering my will and my life to God, I rely on compliance.

I have a plan for my recovery, and I comply with it. I have two home groups: Monday night and Thursday noon. After the Monday night meeting, I go to dinner with the same twelve men. It's my "meeting after the meeting." I rely on them for accurate feedback about me and my recovery. I have a Big Book and a *Twenty-Four Hours a Day* book on my iPhone, my sober friends on speed dial, and a medallion in my pocket, and I use these tools to comply with my program. I comply with my program all the time. With these meetings and these friends, I take the Twelve Steps and practice their principles as a program of recovery. This foundation of compliance is always there for me. On this foundation, I can then build surrender.

SURRENDER

Surrender takes place when our conscious and unconscious minds finally unite in saying yes to recovery. In surrender, we say an unequivocal yes to recovery with our thoughts, our emotions, and our spiritual selves.

In surrender, we no longer entertain drinking or using thoughts. They may come to us, because addiction is a brain disease, but we dismiss them quickly instead of spending loving time with them. For example, I don't seem to have thoughts of whiskey, my favorite drink, but I do have occasional thoughts of white wine. Instead of spending some loving time with those thoughts ("Oh, wouldn't it be nice..."), I just blow off the thoughts as unwanted junk mail of the mind. I have the same emotional response to those thoughts as I do to unwanted telephone solicitations.

In surrender, we are no longer in love with our drugs, including alcohol. We don't romanticize our past relationship with our drug of choice. We don't tell "war stories" about our usage, except when those stories might help another alcoholic or addict recover. We don't relive our past relationship with chemicals for the purpose of rekindling our feelings of attraction to our drugs.

In surrender, our spiritual life is different. Our drugs are no longer our Higher Power. Nor do we live in a universe run by fate, luck, or chance. Even if we have not yet found a good Higher Power, we can sense that the universe is essentially friendly.

We can know we have surrendered when our days are mostly free from struggle. We are no longer fighting anything or anyone, says the Big Book in discussing Step Ten. Love and tolerance of others is our code. When I was living in defiance of God and everyone else, my code was simple: I'm always right. Of course, if I was always right, then you were always wrong, and our conflict was inevitable. In surrender, the code laid out for me is entirely different: love and tolerance. How I apply it is that I love whatever I can possibly love and tolerate whatever I cannot manage to love.

I used to fight everyone and everything, even if a majority of the fights only happened inside my head. I fought traffic, I fought the weather, I fought other employees for raises, I fought other employees for advancement, I fought Congress over political issues—all in my head. Today, when traveling, I sometimes listen to talk radio in the car, just as a reminder, and I hear what the inside of my head used to sound like. Every caller seems mad about something, and it's usually something they cannot control.

HOW TO SURRENDER

Surrender begins as a choice. We make a choice to move away from the expression of our own power and to turn our will and our lives over to the care of our Higher Power. Our natural instincts are to control things. In surrender, we trade in our right to go on controlling our lives, in return for the care of a loving Higher Power. A series of Twelve Step-related bumper stickers, notable for their bright, metal-flaked backgrounds, hold clues to surrender:

"Easy Does It"	"One Day at a Time"
"Live and Let Live"	"Keep It Simple"
"Let Go and Let God"	"Relax, God's in Charge"
"This Too Shall Pass"	"Turn It Over"

What those bumper stickers have in common is that none of them are action steps. None of them are things we can control. There is no bumper sticker that reads, "Grab hold of it and throttle it until it gives up." None of the program slogans have anything to do with exerting our own power over people or events. They all suggest we give our concerns to God, carry our responsibilities, and trust God for the outcome.

TWO LEVELS OF SURRENDER

The basic level of surrender is the one I've just described in which we let go of our resistance to recovery. The more valuable form of surrender is to surrender to God. Bill Wilson did not surrender to recovery, because recovery did not exist. He surrendered to God. His sober friend explained to Bill that he needed a new relationship with his Creator in which he would turn his life over to God's care. Bill Wilson realized that this new relationship with God would come with a price tag: the destruction of his self-centeredness. This key decision made it possible for Bill to go on and become the cofounder of Alcoholics Anonymous. Bill chose to seek God's will for his life and became willing to let go of his self-centeredness. The big surrender, the one that leads through recovery and all the way to happiness, is the one suggested in Step Three: We make a decision to turn our will and our life over to the care of God, as we understand God.

TRUST

As we carry out the decision to surrender to God and put aside our self-centeredness, we develop trust in God. Each time we surrender, and feel the benefits of surrender, our trust grows. Surrender is not an abdication of responsibility. In surrender, we turn our wills and our lives over to the care of God. Our will is our thoughts. Our life is our actions. We turn our thoughts and our actions over to God, doing our very best to separate them from our self-centeredness. In our previous states of defiance, submission, and compliance, we believed that our sense of control and our self-centeredness were getting us the best available results. When we start to get better results through surrender, we are surprised, then pleased; and finally we trust that this new way of life is working.

I used to jam my calendar full of events to wring the maximum results out of my day. I believed that the harder I worked, the more results I would get. As I became more trusting of God and less self-reliant, I put more blank space in my calendar, to leave room for God to put things in my day. At work at Hazelden, I leave my office door open whenever a patient or guest isn't in my office so people can take advantage of a random moment to stop in and ask a question or make a comment. Now that I am certain that God is in charge of my day, I am no longer surprised when the most important things in my day are not on my schedule. How can I possibly know what the most important things are in the coming day? I'm just me. I am not God.

I used to be enraged if an airline flight was canceled, as if my travel plans were infinitely more important than anyone else's. Now, if I am traveling somewhere to speak—which I regard as important—I go a day early so I can be delayed without consequences. If a flight is canceled or rerouted, I just trust that things are working out the way they should. Sometimes I meet someone on the rerouted flight whom I am meant to meet.

One day my Delta flight was canceled, and I was switched to an American Airlines flight two hours later. While I was reading in the gate area, the captain came up to me and introduced himself. He had been a patient at Hazelden and went to treatment during his vacation because he didn't want anyone at the airline to know he had a problem. It was his one-year sobriety anniversary, and he wanted to tell me how happy he was. He was so happy and so enthusiastic that we talked until the plane was all loaded and the gate agent had to prod him to get on board so we could go. He asked if we could keep talking at the destination, and I said, "Sure!"

When I told the story the next week during a patient lecture, a man came up and shook my hand. He thanked me for the story. He was another American Airlines captain, the first to be admitted to Hazelden under a new contract, and he had been feeling miserable. He said, "Thanks, you've given me hope."

Maybe I gave him hope, but first I gave God my schedule. Then God gave me a plane change and introduced me to Captain Tony, who gave me a good story, and then I had a story to pass on. If I got all that from giving God my calendar, then I can trust that I will get a lot more if I turn over more than just my calendar.

DISTRUST

We all have our reasons for distrust. Every time we have been betrayed in life, we have a fresh reason for distrust. We have a bad habit of blaming God for betrayals that were carried out by people. I was betrayed by my mom, who abused me. I was betrayed by the youth minister to whom I turned for help. I was betrayed by pain-killing drugs, which ended up increasing my pain in every way. I was betrayed by alcohol, which offered relief and delivered oppression. I was betrayed by fringe relatives who turned abuse into torture when I was ten and eleven years old and shattered my mind. I was betrayed by my own mind, which delivered inaccurate information about both the past and the present, making it difficult to function. Then, in a final twist, I blamed God for it all—until one day it dawned on me that God had never hit me. Not once. All the bad things in my life had come from the bad will of people and from addiction to alcohol and drugs. Not one bad thing had ever come from God. My surrender was not the surrender of desperation, because I wasn't desperate; I was doing pretty well in sobriety. My surrender was the surrender to the sudden realization that God had been with me all along, not against me.

ACCEPTANCE

Along with the decision to trust God is a decision to practice acceptance. I had already learned from my first sponsor that acceptance did not mean approval; it just meant acceptance of reality. I needed to accept life just the way it was. There's a well-loved sentence in A.A.'s Big Book: "Acceptance is the key to all my problems today" (p. 417). My old way was to fight against my problems, hoping to subdue them. Sometimes that worked. It didn't work on big problems, such as how to recover from alcoholism, from child abuse, and from an unsettled mind. Only when I accepted myself, my problems, and my need to surrender to God did the problems give way.

There is, however, one statement in the Big Book of A.A. that I disagree with: "Nothing, absolutely nothing, happens in God's world by mistake" (p. 417). I believe this sentence is factually incorrect. Auto accidents happen by mistake. Strokes are random events. One in five pregnancies ends in miscarriage. Some negative events are random. To believe otherwise is to make God the author of evil. I hear people in Twelve Step groups say, "God never gives you more than you can handle." That kind of God would be arbitrary and scary, not the gracious Higher Power in whom these programs believe. It would be as if God sat behind a counter, dishing out catastrophes: "Sue's doing OK in recovery, let's break her leg—she can handle it!" Randomness, error, and evil all exist, but they don't come from God.

Acceptance means I accept that all kinds of life events happen, but that in all circumstances, I choose to place myself in God's care and to trust in God. I'm sixty-four years old; I'm not middle aged unless I plan to live to a hundred and twenty-eight. I am aware of death, and I don't have a road map of heaven to reassure me. I accept the existence of death as an abstract concept, but I have plans for next year. How I deal with death is that I trust God to take care of me, now and later, even in death.

Acceptance means I accept people just the way they are right now, not the way they are going to be when I get done changing them. I presided at many weddings during the years I served as a pastor. In premarital counseling I cautioned people that they needed to be ready to make a permanent commitment to the other person just the way he or she was right now, without any plan to make him or her different after marriage. As we explored expectations, it turned out that a lot of people had unexpressed expectations that the other person would later change to suit them.

Somehow, I avoided having expectations that my wife Priscilla would be different than she is. I hoped to marry her long before she even knew I was serious about it. My main reason for wanting to marry her was that I knew she was both kind and good. I didn't yet know why I was seeking those things above all, but I was right in seeking them. She and I are wildly different. She is visually oriented and elegant. I am oriented to sound and space, not how things look, and I am inelegant and a fashion nightmare. Our politics and religion are different, and our ways of being in the world are different. I overplan everything, and she just floats through life, assured that the universe will take care of her. My over-planning usually works well, and the universe does take care of her, even when she pays no attention at all to the plan. By accepting her just the way she is, I have avoided thirty-seven years of arguments, and we've been happier.

LEARNING TO TRUST

Learning to trust came gradually. When I was a child, I learned that life hurt less if I didn't need anything. If food wasn't available, I learned to not be hungry. If I was normally cold, I learned to not feel cold. If there was no human comfort, I learned to be a creature who did not need any comfort, who lived on correct thoughts alone. Where I work today, at Hazelden in Center City, Minnesota, it can be very cold in the winter. If I have to go between buildings when it is well below zero and it's inconvenient to return to my office for a coat, I can still decide to not be cold and can walk three or four minutes in the wind at twenty below zero without feeling any cold or distress. I am aware that if I did it long enough, biology would overcome a rigid mind, but I can still do it for quite a while. In short, I convinced myself deep down that I needed no one, because I had no one. It was a survival tool, and I respect it. The trouble with survival tools is that they don't go away when we no longer need them.

The first clue I remember about the feeling of surrender came when I slipped on the ice and fell many years ago. I was the captain of the rescue squad in my little New England town. I fell on an icy sidewalk and bruised my chest wall and several ribs. I had the wind knocked out of me and had trouble breathing. I couldn't get up and was rescued by my own rescue squad! My first feeling was embarrassment at needing help to get up off the pavement. I expected them to just give me a hand up. However, they came and did a full assessment for broken bones, then carefully shifted me onto a stretcher and took me to the emergency room for X rays. As they were doing this while I was lying there unable to get up, I had the strange feeling of being cared for. When they covered me with blankets, I realized I had been cold. While they sat in the back of the ambulance and joked with me, I realized I had felt alone. Only when I had something could I afford to notice what I didn't have. Only when I came to trust God could I afford to know how hard it was to live entirely on my own.

I learned to distrust very early, just about the time I was learning words, and it was reinforced by reality well into adulthood. Once there were no more people in my life who betrayed me, I was betrayed every day by drugs and alcohol. Chemicals pretended to be my friends, while stripping my life of all its enjoyment. Life's experiences up to age forty, when I got sober, proved that my distrust of people was as well founded and reliable as gravity.

To overcome historical patterns of distrust, we need to try new behaviors and stretch ourselves. I've always loved to travel, but I was afraid to fly. It was an unreasoning, physical fear. I'd get in an airplane to go on vacation, and once in the clouds, I'd have a terrible, gut-wrenching fear that sometime in the next few minutes, we'd all drop like rocks for thousands of feet before being crushed to death in a shattered metal tube. So, I took flying lessons in a single-engine Beechcraft Sport. When I made my solo flight, I felt terrified, but even then I felt less afraid than I had in those commercial airline flights before I learned to fly. Today I love flying. Now that I understand aircraft, they are not scary. I even like those little propeller planes that a lot of people can't stand because I know that propeller planes are actually more "airworthy" than the big jets. I discovered I can learn to trust by taking physical action to overcome my fears.

Opening up free time in my calendar was a physical action. Life went so much better that it helped me trust in God. Now I expect to be in touch with God's will many times during the week. It has led me to a simple, four-part philosophy:

1. Show up.
2. Pay attention.
3. God will do something good.
4. Try to be part of it, or at least admire it when it happens.

I learned about the need for physical trust while listening to a parishioner in one of my churches. She was one of a successful group of teachers who taught in an award-winning junior high school. She told me about a surprise birthday party her friends had held for her. They called ahead of time and asked her if she was available for a surprise party. She asked, "How can it be a surprise party if you're calling me?" They said, "Trust us." I was immediately on high alert at the phrase "trust us"—which was absurd because she was telling me about an event that had already happened, and she was clearly happy about it. On her birthday, they had her wear a bathing suit with shorts and a top over it. They got her in a car and blindfolded her. Then they drove through the White Mountains until she was lost. They walked her through the woods blindfolded for a while. They led her up some steps onto a wooden porch and had her take the shorts and top off, leaving only her bathing suit. Listening to the story, I was getting more anxious—while she was clearly happy. It turned out it wasn't a porch, but a dock. They picked her up, still blindfolded, and launched her out on the lake in an inner tube. Then they all had a picnic and swim party with a group of friends at the lake.

She was perfectly happy telling the story. I was anxious. My conclusion was that it must be nice to be able to trust your friends like that, for I wouldn't know. I later told my friends about my reaction, and they staged a similar birthday surprise for me, but with a different ending. I started out trying to maintain a sense of control while blindfolded but finally gave up and just enjoyed the ride and the "mystery adventure" they had planned. It was my first real experience of letting go of control, and I actually enjoyed it.

SURRENDER, TRUST, AND ACCEPTANCE

Surrender, trust, and acceptance open up a whole new experience of life. As long as we are trying to control life, we automatically limit how much we can enjoy it. Whenever we control life, we are setting limits on it. We set limits to minimize our risk. We never realize that when we limit our risk, we limit our benefit at the same time. Acting out of our self-centeredness, we work hard to achieve mastery. If we are willful enough, and lucky enough, nothing very bad will ever happen to us. The price of that is that nothing very good will ever happen to us either. If we are the only god there is, then we had better be very, very careful. If there is a God who is always present, who is not us, and who will care for us throughout time, then we can take the risk of opening up completely to life, and we will find out everything that is available in this life before it is over.

In surrender, acceptance, and trust, we seek God's protection and care with complete abandon. It would be fun if God would just fill us full of life, as if we were empty vessels, but we have work to do. We are to live our lives by practicing spiritual principles. The next chapter is about practicing those principles.

CHAPTER 4:

PRACTICE WHAT PRINCIPLES?

———

Surrender and trust, which we have just discussed, are traits we can develop in solitude, but further spiritual growth will need to take place in community. The spiritual principles of the Twelve Step programs all take place between and among people, not in isolation. The second half of Step Twelve says "…and practice these principles in all our affairs." That doesn't mean to leave these principles until we are at the end of our program. It means to include these principles in everything we do.

THE PRINCIPLES BEHIND THE STEPS

Recovery comes from taking the Twelve Steps. Each step works because it is grounded in an underlying spiritual principle. A clue to this is found in the wording of Step Twelve, where it says "and practice these principles in all our affairs." It is possible the authors simply meant practicing the steps themselves, but each step has a corresponding spiritual principle.

As we start to get clean and sober, we do the shortest, simplest version of each step. We don't interpret the step— we just do it. If the step says admit, we admit. If the step says make a list, we make a list. Taking the steps is about changing our behavior. A common slogan is "bring your body, and your mind will follow."

It was important for me to do the steps literally, because my alcoholic mind kept looking for loopholes, but as we do the Twelve Steps in cycles over the years, their meaning and purpose deepens, and we find an unending source of spiritual growth. Both of my "home groups" each week are step meetings. At the larger one, we do the cycle of Twelve Steps and then hold a medallion night before beginning the cycle again. One might think that after almost ninety times around the cycle of steps, I would have exhausted their potential, but it was not the potential of the steps that was being explored, it was my potential for spiritual growth throughout my lifetime. Considering my starting point, and how slowly I changed, I have needed all this time to have a life that is sober—and that is becoming happy.

STEP ONE: HONESTY

"We admitted we were powerless over alcohol—that our lives had become unmanageable."

The spiritual principle of Step One is honesty. I began the process of becoming honest by putting a stop to lying. Like many alcoholics, I lied all the time, even when I didn't need to. I lied by reflex. It was as if I had a broken compass. Instead of pointing to true north, my compass pointed to whatever story was likely to keep me out of trouble. My automatic responses were "no" and "I don't know," even if I did know and even if there was no harm in saying "yes." I not only denied my alcoholism, I denied whatever I had just done, sometimes because I couldn't remember it and other times because I thought all questions were part of a plot to uncover my addiction, so I should deny everything just to be safe.

Because the most important thing in my life was obtaining chemicals, using chemicals, minimizing the withdrawal from chemicals, and hiding my addiction to chemicals, telling the truth was a threat, not an asset. Our brains can go on automatic pilot and eliminate even the awareness that we are no longer oriented to the truth.

I drank mostly when my wife wasn't looking. When I drank in her presence, I only had one or two drinks: whiskey sours or gin and tonics. With her I drank harmless little splits of chilled Asti spumante, which hardly have any alcohol at all, served chilled in lovely Waterford cut-glass champagne glasses bought especially for the occasion. I saved the Jack Daniels in a highball glass until after she had gone to bed. She might have known I took Valium and Percodan—I never asked. I went to great lengths to not look or act drunk, which wasn't too hard, considering my high tolerance. It wasn't exactly a lie, it was a deception.

When I was a child, lying was out of place and so it took some sophistication to do it. In our culture now, it seems lying is so normal that honesty is countercultural—it's just that it isn't called lying, or even deception. It's called "spin" or "packaging" or "messaging" or "branding," and people go to school to learn how to do it well. As a culture, we have become used to the idea that no one means what they say. When we telephone a business and are placed on hold, we usually hear, "Your call is important to us…" That's clearly not true, but we wait patiently because we have no choice—if we want to talk to a human, we will wait. If the call were important to them, they would answer it. I know. I have a top-level "black" American Express card. My call actually *is* important to them, so I never get that recording. I still have to punch in my card number, but as soon as I do, a person, not an automated directory or a recording, answers.

"At McDonalds," the sing-song television advertisement says, "we do it all for you." Actually, no. They do it all for them, as they should. McDonald's is a business. They make hamburgers to make money for stockholders, not to feed the poor, so I can't realistically expect them to sit up nights thinking about my needs. The advertising song says they are thinking about me, but I doubt it.

No matter how cynical I get, it's hard to keep up. Best Buy sent me a text message saying I had won a $1,000 gift card. I just had to enter my e-mail address so they could send it to me. It seemed plausible. I had shopped there, so it was possible there was some kind of drawing I had won. The text message said only 118 of the 1,000 cards being awarded were left, so I sent my e-mail address. It turned out I could "win" a $1,000 card only if I signed up for an expensive "Gold Purchasing Plan" and got three of my friends to sign up too. I didn't sign up, but now that I've given them my e-mail, I will probably get spam e-mail forever. I'm not likely to respond to those Nigerian e-mails about $100 million in gold waiting to be freed from a customs shed somewhere if I will just send $3,000 to bribe corrupt customs officials, but this sounded just plausible enough to get me. Fooled again!

In the days of the old Soviet Union, an auto race was held in Vienna with just two cars in it: an American-built Ford and a Russian-built Lada. The Ford beat the Lada. The next day, the Soviet newspaper *Pravda* (the name means "truth") wrote up the race this way: "In the great international Gran Prix Auto Race of Vienna, the Russian-built Lada came in second place.

The American-built Ford came in next to last." The statement was technically true but entirely misleading. My comments were like that. "Have you been drinking?" people would ask. "I only had two drinks!" I'd respond (but if you chew enough Valium with them, it feels like a dozen).

To be sober, we need to be honest. We need to be all the way honest, modified only by kindness. We can't use honesty as an excuse to be cruel to others, but with that exception, we need to be entirely honest. The reason for this is that addiction is a brain disease and our brains are looking for opportunities for self-deception. The disease can present an infinite number of stories and excuses to get us to pick up another addictive drink or drug again, and only rigorous honesty can block them all.

I have taken what may seem an extreme position on honesty, but it works for me. For example, when people say, "How are you?" I don't say "fine" unless I actually am fine. Because of the consequences of child abuse, I am rarely fine. I have chronic pain and trouble sleeping. But the people who ask, "How are you?" don't really want a long story. Most of them are already walking away, so I say something true but short: "fair to partly cloudy" or "sober" or "conscious" or "tired" or "adequate" or "good enough." It's a very minor point, but I don't say "fine" unless I actually am fine.

STEP TWO: HOPE

"Came to believe that a Power greater than ourselves could restore us to sanity."

The spiritual principle of Step Two is hope. I actually took Step Two before I took Step One. I needed to believe that a

Power greater than myself could restore me to sanity before I would ever admit to any weakness at all. To me, the logic was clear: if I am powerless over alcohol and there's no help, I am doomed; so if there is no Higher Power, I am not going to admit to anything. Happily, I did already believe in God, so when I finally woke up to my own powerlessness, I didn't have to search for God.

My previous experience was that God was not necessarily there for me, but the reason I was willing to trust God now and have hope in God was my observation that God was helping other people get and stay sober. We have hope for recovery mostly because we see other people recovering. We want what they have, and we are willing to do what they did to get it.

Hope comes from many sources. I had a friend years ago who was a "low-bottom" drunk. He used to look crazy when he was drunk because he would start bar fights and take on all comers. When the police arrived, he would fight them too. He looked so crazy that the police would stuff him in the state mental hospital instead of taking him to jail. This being the 1970s, it was an old-fashioned mental hospital where they kept you for a while. Late one night, my friend was sitting on a hallway bench, naked and cold, waiting his turn to see the one intake psychiatrist who worked at night. They had taken not only his shoelaces, but everything. He was sitting and talking with another naked, cold guy. The other guy heard his story and said, "You're not crazy, you're an alcoholic. *I'm* crazy." My friend asked what he should do. "When you get out of here, go to A.A. That's for alcoholics. This place is for crazy people." My friend followed the advice and got sober. Once sober, he didn't pick fights, and he came to believe that a Power greater than himself could restore him to sanity, because he *was* being restored to sanity.

Narcotics Anonymous has a straightforward statement of hope. Their primary purpose, they state, is that "no addict seeking recovery need die." That is wonderfully hopeful and defiant at the same time. We challenge this disease head on. We believe in the power of God, and we commit ourselves to the battle against addiction—with great hope.

A.A. has a responsibility pledge: "I am responsible. When anyone, anywhere, reaches out for help, I want the hand of A.A. always to be there. And for that, I am responsible." We trust God and do our part in hopeful cooperation.

Thirty-eight thousand patients have come through residential treatment since I started working at Hazelden–Center City. The stories of hope could fill volumes. This one stands out, though, perhaps because our staff did so little that it's clear God did a lot:

Hazelden reserves some free beds for use by the government of Chisago County, where we are located. We want to be of service to people of low income and no income right next door. A county health worker would walk through the jail and ask people if they wanted to go to treatment. If they said anything other than "yes," he kept walking. A patient I called "Bill the Cat" said yes.

The original Bill the Cat was a cartoon character in a strip called *Bloom Country*. Bill the Cat was a cat that looked like he had been run over by a steamroller: bewildered, shocked, hair sticking up. That's how our Bill looked. He was malnourished and nearly unresponsive from drinking and not eating. He lived in a broken-down tow truck he had formerly operated. He would leave his dead tow truck long enough to steal something or forge checks, buy drugs and alcohol, and crawl back in it to sleep. He got arrested here and there, all for petty crimes. He was so sickly that I think even the jail didn't want him, and we got him.

Bill came to the Silkworth unit from the medical unit and was barely aware of his surroundings. The men of Silkworth were kind to him and guided him to meals, lectures, and groups, but it wasn't clear if he even knew where he was. After five days, an arrest warrant arrived from Dakota County, and off he went.

The judge in Dakota County, seeing that he had come from Hazelden, continued his case without a finding and sent him back. The Silkworth men welcomed him back and made sure he ate and slept. After ten days, he knew he was in treatment. Then a warrant came from Anoka County, and he left. The Anoka judge continued his case without a finding, and Bill came back. After twenty-one days, Bill figured out he was an alcoholic, and at the end of his twenty-eight-day treatment, he was ready for treatment—except that his time was up.

We got him a free space at Hazelden–Saint Paul's Fellowship Club, and he went to the halfway house there. He got into A.A. and into a counseling group. At Fellowship Club, you are supposed to get a job. Bill's driver's license was long since revoked, but he got a job with a major towing company doing unlocks of locked cars because he could get into any locked vehicle without damaging it.

It's years later, and Bill's white hair is salt-and-pepper colored. His mind is alert; he's sober and happy. He has his own apartment, he's making his A.A. meetings and still doing unlocks for the towing company. This is the kind of miracle that makes me sure God is with us, and Bill's story tells me there is hope for everyone.

STEP THREE: FAITH

*"Made a decision to turn our will and
our lives over to the care of
God as we understood Him."*

The spiritual principle of Step Three is faith. The step asks us to make a decision to turn our will and our life over to the care of "God *as we understood Him.*" That requires some faith in God or a Higher Power. In "Bill's Story," chapter 1 of the A.A.'s Big Book, Bill wrote:

> *My friend suggested what then seemed a novel idea. He said, "Why don't you choose your own conception of God?"...It was only a matter of being willing to believe in a Power greater than myself. Nothing more was required of me to make my beginning. (p. 12)*

It seems Step Three is a point at which our addictions make a strong counterattack, for if we develop faith in a Higher Power, we are likely to overcome the addictions. At this point, all manner of skepticism and newly found caution develops. We did not have any of these objections to faith when we had faith in alcohol or drugs.

One of the things I get to do on the Silkworth men's unit at Hazelden is the weekly Step Two and Three group. In that group, I get to hear all the sudden anxieties that come up when patients are about to develop faith in God, a Higher Power, their peers, Hazelden, or recovery. People ask how they can have faith in God because I cannot prove that God is real. I say, "That's nothing—once you leave the room, I can't prove that *you* are real, either."

I understand that there's no proof of God's existence, but there's no proof of Jack Daniels's existence, either, and yet I drank his whiskey.

I was never troubled by these thoughts. I never questioned how sound my thinking was when I went to Al-Anon to find a codependent physician's assistant who would write me all the prescriptions I wanted. I peeled off all those little colored labels on the pill bottles that said "DO NOT MIX WITH ALCOHOL" because I thought they were just advisory. I never questioned that.

Once I had a Silkworth patient who seemed depressed. His counselor sent him to the mental health clinic. He came back with a prescription for Prozac. The patient said, "I'm not going to take Prozac. I read in the *Wall Street Journal* that Prozac can have dangerous side effects." The counselor said, "Listen to yourself. You're a heroin addict. When did you start worrying about dangerous drugs?"

We willingly take all kinds of risks to support our addiction, but balk at having some faith in God. It's time to do it if we want to be well.

STEP FOUR: COURAGE

"Made a searching and fearless moral inventory of ourselves."

The spiritual principle of Step Four is courage. The step invites us to take a searching and fearless moral inventory of ourselves. To do so requires courage.

I never went to treatment, so there was no timetable for my recovery. I just went to meetings. My sponsor was in no hurry for me to move ahead to the next step until I had thoroughly taken the step before it, so I had no time pressure to take Step Four. I put it off because I was afraid to take it. Part of the problem was that I didn't remember a lot of my past. I didn't know if it was missing due to blackouts or trauma or simply the selfishness of not wanting to remember painful and embarrassing things. I was just afraid to find out what was wrong with me.

I thought Step Four presented me with a loophole. I thought of courage as the absence of fear. Because I was still afraid, I figured I was not ready to take this step. The trouble was that years went by and fear remained, so there was no readiness to take the step. Nothing was available to break the deadlock.

Finally I decided to redefine courage as not the absence of fear but the willingness to go ahead and do the right thing, even while afraid. If we think about the common context of fear—wartime—it becomes clear. The hero who gets a medal for courage in battle might well be afraid, but the hero does the right thing despite the fear. So, we pick up pen and paper and take our own inventory.

Courage is needed for many things. We need courage to face life on life's terms, without illusion or fantasy. We need courage to develop the part of us that remains undeveloped: our capacity for feeling and expressing emotion, or our capacity for calm, steady responses to life, or our reliable focus on service to others—whatever hasn't been there that should be present in our lives.

I now live in Minnesota. There are a lot of Scandinavian jokes. Some are about a cultural difficulty with expressing emotion. There's a joke about the old Norwegian man who loved his wife so much, he almost told her. We laugh at the stereotype, but we alcoholics, who had no trouble expressing our anger when we were drunk, often are stuck and speechless when it comes to expressing love and heartfelt affection in sobriety.

Courage allows us to walk not around our troubles but straight toward them, in the company of God and our recovering friends, in order to overcome them. There are many "brands" of spirituality that consider trouble an illusion, something we can wipe away. The Twelve Step programs have a spirituality that allows us to see reality clearly, face it, and live with acceptance of our lives and our character defects. Carl Jung, the psychiatrist who corresponded with Bill Wilson, once wrote, "One does not become enlightened by imagining figures of light, but by making the darkness conscious." Taking our own inventory, with courage, and knowing that there is a Fifth Step to come, puts us on the path of enlightenment.

Sometimes courage means confronting something inside ourselves; sometimes courage means confronting something outside ourselves. On September 11, 2001, Stephen Adams died in the terrorist attacks on the World Trade Center in New York. His brother Lawrence promised himself that if something like that ever happened near him, he would "never hide under a table." Ten and a half years later, when Lawrence was fifty-six, he was in Café Racer in Seattle when a disturbed man armed with two .45-caliber handguns began shooting people, killing four. Lawrence, unarmed, picked up a series of stools and hurled then at the gunman, striking him repeatedly while other people took the chance to run out the door. The gunman finally ran away. By doing this, Lawrence saved several lives. He somehow managed to avoid being shot himself. I don't know if he was in recovery, but he was a fine example of courage: doing the right thing and saving lives when he had a good reason to be afraid.

STEP FIVE: INTEGRITY

"Admitted to God, to ourselves, and to another human being the exact nature of our wrongs."

The spiritual principle of Step Five is integrity. In this instance, integrity does not use the common meaning, which is almost the same as honesty. The integrity of Step Five is wholeness. An integer is a whole number, not a fraction. As we take Step Five, our fractured and fractional lives come together, and we have the opportunity to become whole again. We have the opportunity to have integrity.

In Step Five we are asked to admit to God, to ourselves, and to one other human being the exact nature of our wrongs. The usual expectation for this step is that we will unburden ourselves and will then get a sense of relief. This often happens. In addition, another, more important dynamic is at work.

Before we take our Fifth Step, we alcoholics and addicts have maintained an alibi system, a set of lies and deceptions intended to protect the secret of our alcoholism and addiction. We developed a pervasive dishonesty that drew attention away from addiction and diverted it onto other people and other circumstances to keep the truth from ever coming out.

To better hide the truth, I created a set of fake, fractional selves, each of whom looked sober, or sober enough, to pass as a competent adult. It was as if I made cardboard cutouts of fake selves and sent them out to meet the world.

When I was a child, there were photographers in Times Square who had cardboard cutouts of the current president. For five dollars, you could get your picture taken with the cardboard president, and the resulting photo would look like you were shaking the president's hand in Times Square. In the fall of 2011, the Minnesota Democratic Party would have liked to have President Obama stand in its booth at the state fair for twelve days to meet the public, but he wasn't available. So the party had a lovely cardboard cutout of President Obama on hand to meet the public. I have a great photo of myself and the cardboard president shaking hands at the fair.

I was a cardboard man myself when I had no integrity. I sent a cardboard cutout of a good husband home to meet my wife and a cardboard cutout of a good father to meet my children. I sent a cardboard cutout of a sober minister into the pulpit of the church and put a cardboard cutout of a good citizen behind the wheel of my car—and I hoped no one would ever notice the fearful drunk behind those cutouts.

It's a lot of work keeping track of all our cardboard cutouts, especially if they talk a lot while drunk. We have to remember what they said, what they promised, the appointments or dates they made, where they've been, and with whom. This is even harder if our real self, the alcoholic who no one sees, has blackouts and memory lapses.

Before we take Step Five, most of us don't admit to having wrongs or to being wrong, because if we admit to being wrong in any area of life, then the whole set of lies and deception may come crashing down. Being a fractional self is hard because we have to try to make sense out of all the nonsense our fractional selves have said and done.

When we take Step Five, we admit the exact nature of our wrongs. The relief comes because we finally admit that we *have* wrongs. We *have* wrongs, and we *are* wrong sometimes. Now we don't need all the fake-perfect selves anymore. We can be whole people, a genuine mixture of good and bad.

A.A. says, "We claim spiritual progress, not spiritual perfection." We can discard the cardboard cutouts. We can integrate all our fractional selves and have integrity as whole people, with both our good points and our bad points.

In the past, no one got to see beyond my cardboard. Now there is just one me. The John who wrote this book is the same John my wife gets at home, the same John the airline ticket clerk meets, and the same John people get when I lecture. Now, if what I say today doesn't match what I said yesterday, it is because I changed my mind—it isn't because I can't keep my lies together. This is a big relief. Integrity is letting go of all pretenses and just being who we are.

STEP SIX: WILLINGNESS

"Were entirely ready to have God remove all these defects of character."

The spiritual principle of Step Six is willingness. We need to become willing to be changed, or our recovery will come to a halt. Notice that I did not say we need to become willing to change ourselves. We become willing to have our Higher Power change us. Our willingness to change is a beginning. The serenity prayer includes the phrase "the courage to change the things I can." Taking the Twelve Steps involves a personal willingness to change.

Our power has limits. One unvarying limit is that we are powerless over alcohol or powerless over addiction. So not only do we need our own willingness, we also must become willing to have our Higher Power change us in ways we do not yet know. This combined willingness is a bit like writing a blank check.

When we begin, we do not know where it will all end, and we don't have an awareness of where all this change will lead us.

A brief summary of spiritual principles in the A.A.'s Big Book is the acronym HOW, which stands for honest, open, and willing. We are invited to apply the concept of HOW to every area of life: How to get sober? Honestly, openly, and willingly. How to have a relationship? Honestly, openly, and willingly. How to apply for a job? Honestly, openly, and willingly. Willingness to change and willingness to be changed in all areas of life—willingness that is well informed by our inventory—can be a powerful force that will propel us forward in recovery. It is powerful because it propels us straight toward God, by whom we can be transformed.

Step Six says we were entirely ready to have God remove all these defects of character. That requires our willingness. My experience was that I was somewhat ready to have God remove my character defects, and God somewhat did. My first attempt at Step Five still had too much about other people in it, and so did my first Sixth Step, too. I was only willing to have some of my character defects removed because other people in my life hadn't been willing to have their character defects removed and I didn't want to be at too much of a competitive disadvantage to them. Besides, I kind of liked my character defects. I thought my defects were assets. I thought my character defects added a sense of color and personality spark to an otherwise bland existence. I thought my sarcasm was a talent to be cultivated. I thought that quick wit and the ability to go on the attack in an instant was a good career move. I had insults ready on standby, such as, "If I throw a bone, will you leave?" I had no idea that my prickly personality, which was intended to protect me from being picked on, also "protected" me from friendship, intimacy, closeness, and trust. My initial experience with Step Six was that I would get a little bit willing to let God change me, and God would make a little change in me. Yet even the little change felt good.

One of the program slogans says, "Let go and let God." As I stopped rationing change and stopped controlling what I would let God do in my heart, I started to feel better. Instead of deciding, bit by grudging bit, what I would change, often at the urging of my sponsor and program friends, I learned to welcome changes from God, without knowing in advance what those changes would be. Finally, when Step Six came around again in the rotation of step meetings, I could ask God to remove defects of character that I could not even name but needed to be removed. At that point, a great relief came over me, and I could feel my resistance and resentment flowing out of me.

Now my willingness has become eagerness, because every time I have been willing to be changed by God and every time I have experienced God changing me, it has been for the better. This willingness is a lot like surrender. The struggle is gone, and we can just let go and enjoy the process.

STEP SEVEN: HUMILITY

"Humbly asked Him to remove our shortcomings."

The spiritual principle of Step Seven is humility. The step says we humbly asked God to remove our shortcomings. It may be a measure of our spiritual progress that the names given to our problems seem to soften as we move through these steps. Step Five talks about "our wrongs." Step Six refers to "defects of character." Step Seven speaks of our "shortcomings" being removed. Perhaps as we move through the steps and move toward letting go of our wrongs, they are being softened.

Humility is not the same as humiliation. Humiliation is being put down by someone else. Humility is having a true and accurate perspective about ourselves, as we are taught in these Twelve Step programs. What these programs teach me about myself is that I am the equal of every other man and woman. I am not better than anyone, but I am also not worse than anyone. We are all children of God and all loved equally. In these programs, we are all addicts because we all have the same type of brain disorder. The kind of drugs we favor varies, but we are all addicts. This is a vital spiritual truth, and without it I am unlikely to stay sober because I will become either grandiose or hopeless.

Depending on our starting point, we may need to step up to become humble, or we may need to step down to become humble. The grandiose person needs to step down, by disciplining his or her ego. The despairing person needs to step up, by grabbing hold of hope and claiming his or her place in recovery.

We find it amusing when grandiose people have to step down. In 1968, I worked part time in Stern Brothers' Department Store in Woodbridge, New Jersey. This was in a time before computers, cell phones, pagers, and electronic cash registers. Sales slips were multicolored pads of paper with carbon paper between the sheets to make copies: a white customer copy, a green cash register copy, a pink shipping copy, and a tan accounting copy.

It was during the Christmas rush, and I was taking a phone order for eighteen sets of cheap coasters that sold for $9.99 a set. The caller wanted each set gift wrapped with gold bows, a Christmas card written out for each set, and each set mailed to a different name and address. During the process, I mentioned that there would be a $3.00 shipping charge on each one, because free shipping was for items of $10.00 or more. At the mention of the shipping charges, my caller flew into a rage. My recollection is that it went something like this:

Caller: "You will not charge me three dollars each! I am a vice president of Allied Stores. We OWN Stern Brothers. I am a great merchant prince. Fleets of ships sail at my very command. I hire and fire people every day, do business in the millions, and I could have your job like THAT!" (I thought, You wouldn't like my job.) "EVERYONE in the company does what I say and YOU WILL TOO! DO YOU UNDERSTAND WHO YOU ARE TALKING TO?"

I said, "Yes, sir, you are a vice president of Allied Stores. You own Stern Brothers. You are a great merchant prince. Fleets of ships sail at your very command. You hire and fire and buy and sell and do business in the millions, but all that is as nothing." Then I shouted as loud as I could, "DO YOU KNOW WHO THIS IS?"

He said, "No."

I said, "Good" and hung up.

Just as we find it amusing when grandiose people are forced to confront the limits of their own grandiosity and step down a notch, we need to develop the same joy and happiness when formerly despairing people claim their right to exist and their right to recover. They come to a meeting and say, "Hi! I'm me, and I'm an alcoholic, and I want what you have!" We go, "Yes!" and celebrate the fact that another suffering alcoholic has claimed his or her place in recovery.

There is tremendous freedom in humility. The alcoholic is often correctly identified as an egomaniac with an inferiority complex. When I was drinking, I felt like an impostor. I thought that social or academic standing would treat these feelings of being a fraud. I thought that becoming an ordained minister would help me feel like somebody, but it did not. I thought that getting a doctoral degree in ministry and specializing in family therapy would make me feel like somebody. I thought that being Dr. MacDougall would make me feel like being somebody in a way that being John didn't. Nothing changed. The feelings of being an impostor were not caused by a lack of titles or achievements. The feelings of being an impostor were caused by actually *being* an impostor. The feelings were accurate because behind the titles and roles, the truth was I was a drunk and a pill popper. The feelings wouldn't go away, because they were true.

Now, when I say, "Hi, I'm John, and I'm an alcoholic," I feel no sense of disgrace, only freedom. I am merely stating things that are absolutely true. In the programs of A.A., N.A., and Al-Anon, I find I am completely welcome on that basis. I need no degrees, no status, and no employment to be accepted. I am free. We are all free to be accepted in our humility, our equality, and our humanity.

We are grateful to be accepted the way we are, with our shortcomings, but we are not content to live with our shortcomings unchallenged. We have asked God to remove our shortcomings. When we ask God to remove our shortcomings, God gives us homework to do. We take pen and paper and begin to take the Eighth Step.

STEP EIGHT: COMPASSION

"Made a list of all persons we had harmed, and became willing to make amends to them all."

In Step Eight, we make a list of all persons we have harmed and become willing to make amends to them all. To do this, we need to develop compassion, the spiritual principle for this step. To get a complete list of all persons we have harmed, we have to notice that we have harmed them.

My original Eighth Step list was short. I made a list of persons I had harmed who didn't deserve it. The list was short because I thought most people I'd harmed had it coming to them, so I was justified in harming them. If I was justified in harming them, then they didn't belong on my list, and there was no use wasting my valuable time and attention on people who didn't deserve it. I was using righteousness as my guide, not compassion. I was only looking at whether my actions could be justified and not looking at the pain and suffering my words and actions caused.

My first sponsor taught me to take each word of each step and read it exactly as it sits on the page, without interpreting it. Only after I have read the plain meaning and carried out the step exactly as it reads am I free to think about the broader implications. This was wise, because whenever I began to interpret the steps, I always twisted them to serve me, not God or other people.

The step says, "all persons we had harmed." It doesn't differentiate between people we righteously harmed and those we harmed without any possible justification. Only with compassionate hearts can we understand this. Guilty people suffer just as much as innocent ones when they are harmed. When I am sarcastic to a guilty person who I imagine "has it coming to them," the wound hurts just as much as if I had been sarcastic to an innocent person.

As I said, my first Step Eight list was short. It consisted of people I had harmed on purpose who didn't deserve it. My second Step Eight list was a bit longer. It included all people I had harmed on purpose. My third list included people I had harmed by mistake, as well as those I had harmed on purpose. My fourth Step Eight list included people I had harmed on purpose, people I had harmed by mistake, and people I had harmed by omission by leaving out something I should have done.

My memory of when the following incident happened is unclear, but my memory of what happened is clear and painful. My wife was driving my older daughter to the airport when she was a young adult and no longer lived with us. As they went out the kitchen door, I turned to my older daughter and said, "I love you." It seemed appropriate at the time. My wife returned hours later and said, "Oh, she cried all the way to the airport." I asked why, because all I'd said was, "I love you." My wife said, "Yes, but you've never said it before."

I thought I'd been a good enough father by being steady and reliable. I had been consistent and provided structure. I had taught my daughters a lot of things and prepared them to be competent adults. I hadn't noticed that I'd left something out: love and affection. Leaving love and affection out was a wrong by omission. Now it is years later, and I never leave her or sign off on the phone without saying I love her. It's a small amends, but over time it adds up to something.

We can have compassion even toward those who have wronged us. I had a lot of anger and resentment toward my mother for my child abuse, but as this recovery program has changed me, I have found compassion even for her. I once wrote a letter to her, after her death, to help myself with my feelings. As I wrote, a sentence emerged that surprised me: "As much as it hurts to be a little boy whose mommy hates him, it must also hurt to be a woman who hates her little boy." I began to imagine what it must have been like to go through an unwanted pregnancy and give birth to a child who reminded you of a husband you hated. I imagined how painful it would be to have to raise that child while hating him so much that your hatred exploded into abuse, and then to live out your lifetime of eighty-six and a half years with all your hatred intact, fresh as new.

STEP NINE: JUSTICE

"Made direct amends to such people wherever possible, except when to do so would injure them or others."

The spiritual principle of Step Nine is justice. The step invites us to make direct amends to the people we have harmed. The step leaves open the exception for when our direct amends would injure them or others.

My first reading of each step was a diligent search for the loopholes that would allow me to recover without doing any actual work. I seized on the exception for where the amends would injure others. I decided I was one of those others. Then I took an expansive view of what constituted an injury. When I put those together, I concluded that any action that might cause me distress constituted an injury to myself and thus I need not do it. I did not want to face the pain of knowing I had been unjust. H. L. Mencken, my favorite newspaper writer, once wrote, "Injustice may sting, but what *really* stings is justice." I only wanted justice where I had been the victim, and I was much less interested in justice where I was in the wrong. Walking through that giant loophole would allow me to completely miss the point of this step and never get its spiritual benefit. The point of the step is justice, and justice is actually good for us.

It is not enough to stop committing injustice. We need to actively commit justice. That is, we need to deliberately seek out ways we have been participating in injustice and then try to set them right. If we have been victims of injustice, we can remain victims and keep our grievances fresh, or we can work to establish justice in the world wherever we can, and in doing so we help heal ourselves.

I was briefly the manager of another department at Hazelden. I had reason to believe I would be the manager of that department for only a few months before it would be transferred to someone else. I tried to run it well and look for improvements that could be carried out in a month or two. The department had an administrative assistant who did a great deal of work. She was essential to the good operation of the department. She was, in effect, the department memory and nerve center. She made it run. Because she had been hired a long time ago at a very low pay grade, she had gotten only the small annual increases, and her pay was well below that of people currently being hired for similar jobs in other departments. I pressed hard to have her pay adjusted to a level near the top of the scale because her work was at the top of the scale. I got her a 32 percent raise in the middle of the year. One of my happiest moments at Hazelden was when she said to me, "A lot of managers have said they'd try to do something for me, but you actually did." Two weeks later, in a move that had been planned all along, the department was reassigned to another manager. I was happy to have brought some justice into her life during my short tenure.

It is good for our spiritual growth to examine our own consciences for injustice. Are we unfair to anyone? Have we prejudged anyone? Do we automatically distrust one race, one type of person, one group, without getting to know the individual? Do we favor one of our children over another in our behavior toward them? Are we unfair at work in a way that provokes conflict? How are we doing at placing principles above personalities?

Becoming just is a lot like becoming honest. Making the decision to become just is crucial. It is a big change from our addictive way of life, but it is worth it. Making the change takes practice until it becomes natural. Once we have made the shift, it becomes effortless, and it fills life with ease and happiness.

STEP TEN: PERSEVERANCE

"Continued to take personal inventory, and when we were wrong, promptly admitted it."

The spiritual principle of Step Ten is perseverance. As we take Step Ten, we are continuing to take our personal inventory, and when we are wrong, promptly admitting it. The step doesn't specify every day, but nearly everyone who is regularly taking this step says to take it every day or else on a continuous basis, moment by moment. This behavior requires perseverance.

The reason we have to take the Tenth Step every day is that our disease is active every day. This is partly because it is a brain disease and the alcoholic thinking is part of our thinking every day. Another reason is found in the second law of general systems theory: the unavailability of energy in a closed system. This law holds that everything in the entire universe has an inherent tendency to slow down, stop moving, and become the same temperature as its surroundings unless the system is opened up and fresh energy is introduced. A simple example is a car. It is a closed system. Unless we remove the gas cap, making it an open system, and introduce new energy in the form of gasoline, the car will slow down, stop moving, and become the same temperature as its surroundings. So it is with our recovery. Unless we open our minds and take in fresh energy for recovery, in the form of Step Ten, as well as other steps, meetings, prayer and meditation, and other forms of fresh energy, our recovery will slow down, stop, and become lukewarm. The practice of introducing fresh energy into our recovery on a daily basis is perseverance.

The simplest form of Step Ten asks us to admit when we are wrong. As we read the Big Book text, we find four suggestions about what to do when selfishness, dishonesty, resentment, or fear shows up in us:

> *We ask God at once to remove them. We discuss them with someone immediately and make amends quickly if we have harmed anyone. Then we resolutely turn our thoughts to someone we can help. (p. 84)*

If it weren't for the chronic nature of alcoholism and addiction, this could well be a ten-step program, not a twelve-step one. But remember, we admitted we were powerless over alcohol or addiction and that our lives had become unmanageable. Our perseverance is not enough to ensure a lifetime of sobriety. We need a Power much greater than ourselves, and we need conscious contact with God *as we understand God.*

STEP ELEVEN: SPIRITUAL AWARENESS

"Sought through prayer and meditation to have conscious contact with God as we understood Him, praying only for knowledge of His will for our lives, and the power to carry that out."

The spiritual principle of Step Eleven is spiritual awareness. The step asks us to both pray and meditate. The Twelve Step programs don't tell us how to pray. Even when prayers are written out in program literature, they are not prescribed. The Step Seven prayer in A.A.'s Big Book is widely used, but even there the book says, "When ready, we say something like this." The book doesn't say, "Pray this prayer." Prayer is simply talking to our Higher Power. Meditation is simply listening. We can pray any way we want to. When we are done expressing ourselves, it is a good idea to listen. How well would any human relationship go if we only spoke and then walked away without listening? When we combine prayer with meditation, we maximize the chance that we will have conscious contact.

The step suggests that we pray for two things: knowledge of God's will for our lives and the power to carry it out. This is treatment for the spiritual heart of our illness. Much is said about the neurological basis of addiction, how that brain disease manifests itself in a profound selfishness. Praying all through the day to be shown what God wants us to do is an effective treatment for brains that can only perceive what they want. If we develop a rhythm of moving between praying for knowledge of God's will and meditating on God's will, we can gently rock ourselves out of the rut of self-seeking and self-soothing.

Getting stuff has a limited satisfaction. I was at a meeting one evening where a man was reflecting on his story of recovery, relapse, and recovery. He said: "When I grew up, I got a job, a wife, a house, a car, and a drinking problem. I lost the job, the wife, the house, the car, and I kept the drinking problem. Then I got sober, and I got another job, another wife, another house, another car, and I'm about to get another drinking problem, but it's dawning on me that life is more than just a scavenger hunt."

We all have immediate needs. Some of them need to be tended to immediately. We've already agreed that sobriety must come first. Sobriety is more than not drinking. Sobriety includes spiritual awareness, which is the awareness that knowing and doing God's will for us in this moment is the only thing worth doing. If we are spiritually aware enough to put that ahead of everything, we finally get the full value out of everything we do. We may already have had the opportunity to become happy, but prayer and meditation on the theme of God's will for our lives and the power to carry it out turns the *opportunity* to become happy into the *reality* of being happy.

STEP TWELVE: SERVICE

"Having had a spiritual awakening as the result of these steps, we tried to carry this message to alcoholics, and to practice these principles in all our affairs."

The spiritual principle of Step Twelve is service. Service flows as a natural response to gratitude. Gratitude comes as we realize that our recovery is not an achievement but a gift from God.

Back at Step Three, we made a decision to turn our wills and our lives over to the care of God *as we understood him*. I'm not sure we understand God a whole lot better now at Step Twelve than we did back at Step Three. Step Twelve reveals what has happened to us as a natural result of what we have done and what our Higher Power has done for us: we have had a spiritual awakening as the result of these steps.

At this point, there is still an opportunity to avoid a spiritual awakening by letting our selfishness back into our programs. We do this by taking credit for our recovery. If we believe our recovery is our achievement, then we can be proud of it and it belongs to us. If it is our achievement and we are proud of it, then it is up to us to maintain it, and we go forward, armed with our own self-will. Our self-will is subject to the law of entropy and to the inherent weaknesses of human beings, and it will eventually fail.

If, instead of seeing our recovery as our achievement, we see our recovery as a gift from our Creator, then we will be grateful for the gift. We will guard it, maintain it, and nurture it. We will be happy to engage in service to others, knowing that service to others helps preserve the gift for us.

Some service is easy, some is hard. I enjoy speaking, but I find writing to be difficult and slow. My favorite thing to do is speak at an A.A. roundup. So far, I have spoken at A.A. round-ups in Aspen, Colorado, and Las Vegas and Reno, Nevada. Speaking to a crowd of hundreds or thousands of alcoholics who want you to succeed is a great energy rush, and it's fun, too. That service is easy. I'm a natural speaker. I'm not a natural writer. I'm writing this book, even though it comes slowly and with difficulty, because I want to be of service to people I will never meet. If readers can get a few ideas out of this book that they can use to make their lives better, I will consider that a "win" for the book and a useful service.

Our recovery is a gift. We didn't get the gift because we were lucky or because God likes us better than God likes the alcoholics and addicts who still suffer. We got this gift for a purpose. That purpose is to stay sober and help others achieve sobriety. As we pass on sobriety, our own sobriety is increased. In giving, we get more. God's arithmetic is strange, but it is wonderful.

The recovery comedian, Mark Lundholm, says of the alcoholic in early recovery: "First thought-Wrong!" As we practice these principles, daily and hourly, our first thoughts finally become right.

CHAPTER 5:

SPIRITUAL RECOVERY FROM
TRAUMA AND ABUSE

A chapter on trauma and abuse seems like it doesn't belong in a book on becoming happy, but for those who have been abused or traumatized, happiness will be forever elusive if we do not face the truth about ourselves. If you need to skip over this chapter, do so, but find someone safe with whom you can talk about your feelings.

WHAT DO TRAUMA/ABUSE HAVE TO DO WITH ALCOHOLISM/ADDICTION?

Alcoholism and abuse are separate issues. One doesn't cause the other, and recovery from one does not bring about recovery from the other. But issues of abuse and trauma exist in the lives of a great many alcoholics and addicts. The most obvious connection is that some of us, myself included, began using alcohol and drugs to treat the pain of abuse. We got trapped in addiction because the drugs seemed to work. We were in unbearable pain, and our drugs of choice made the pain bearable. Some of our drug mixtures made the pain stop. Other drug mixtures left us still in pain, but drugged enough that we felt a kind of relief.

By the time I started fifth grade in school, my abuse was severe enough that I would sit in the classroom crying and shaking. The teacher sent me to the nurse. The nurse sent me to my family doctor. I was malnourished, I had migraine headaches, I had chronic pain, and I was extremely anxious. So the doctor gave me a milkshake called Sustagen, which had a day's nutrition in a can, Fiorinal (a barbiturate) with codeine (an opiate) for migraines, Percodan (an opiate with aspirin) for pain, and Librium (an addictive tranquilizer) for anxiety. Later, when my mind snapped from being tortured, I was further given Thorazine, an addictive antipsychotic drug. I was already drinking whiskey out of my parents' supply. Their supply was large enough and flowed fast enough that they never noticed my diversion from it.

I stopped shaking and crying in school, and the medications were considered a success. I continued to be abused, but I didn't show many outward signs of stress. Society was relieved of the distress of seeing a crying and shaking child.

My story is common. People like me are in every Twelve Step meeting. Once I was invited to lead a three-day men's A.A. retreat. The topic was rigorous honesty. One of my talks was on the A.A. saying that "we are only as sick as our secrets." It was the custom on this A.A. group's retreat that participants could sign up for fifteen-minute individual visits with the retreat leader. All sixty-one men signed up for fifteen-minute interviews, which meant fifteen hours and fifteen minutes of fifteen-minute interviews, which made for an exhausting three-day weekend.

The men knew their time was short, so they came in and got right to the point. None of them raised the issue of abuse. However, almost half of them made what I call "doorknob comments." As they were leaving, often with a hand on the doorknob, they would say something like, "There's this other issue I ought to talk about, but we don't have time." Then they would leave. I had a good guess what the other issue was.

At dinner the second evening, I announced that we would hold an extra meeting after the evening session, on the lower level of the retreat center, on the topic of abuse. I would conduct it like a Twelve Step meeting. I would open by briefly qualifying as an abuse survivor, and then I would pass. We would go around the group, and anyone with something to say could say it once or pass. No feedback, no cross talk, and no advice. When we had gone around the circle once, we would say the serenity prayer, and the session would be over.

Twenty-eight men out of the sixty-one attendees came downstairs at 10:30 p.m. Most said something they had never told anyone. Some cried. Some raged. Some made flat statements that entirely hid their feelings. It took us four hours and ten minutes to tell our stories. We finished at 2:40 a.m. When we went upstairs, most of the other men were waiting for us. They sensed that something terribly important was going on. It was.

THE POWER OF TELLING THE TRUTH

What I learned that night was that we have tremendous power for healing when we gather together as recovering people and tell each other the truth. What truth shall we tell?

When we are forced to endure what we cannot endure, something breaks inside our minds. That broken-mindedness is commonly called trauma. There is a psychological diagnosis called "post-traumatic stress disorder" (PTSD), which says if someone is still showing symptoms of brokenness more than six months after a traumatic event, then it is a psychological disorder. My response to that is, "Of course!" Broken people tend to stay broken unless there is a program of healing.

The traumatic event can be a one-time thing or a long process. The destruction of the World Trade Center in New York was a one-time event, but there are people with lifelong nightmares from it. Repeated tours of duty as a soldier in Iraq or Afghanistan is a series of traumas that go on for years, and the "disorder" that follows can actually be a natural reaction to the horror the soldier has lived through.

A category of psychological disorder that has never been officially adopted is "complex post-traumatic stress disorder." It was suggested by Judith Lewis Herman, MD, in her book *Trauma and Recovery*. She suggested it would apply to children who had to grow up while being traumatized. The soldier who is traumatized at least had a chance to develop a personality before being traumatized. The child who is abused has to form a personality for the first time while being abused, a process somewhat like trying to fix a car's automatic transmission while the car is moving.

Trauma is being forced to endure what we cannot endure. Usually the thing we cannot endure is an event or a series of events that are shocking to the normal conscience. However, a child can be traumatized by what doesn't happen, as well. Alice Miller, a Swiss child psychiatrist, wrote, "The greatest injury a child can have is to never be loved just the way they are." Neglect and complete indifference to the life of a child can be just as traumatizing as any assault.

To recover from alcoholism, we have to admit we have it. That is why, in every A.A. meeting, we begin by saying, "Hi! I'm John, and I'm an alcoholic." After we have heard hundreds of people introduce themselves as alcoholics, we can hardly be surprised that the next person does so too. So why do we do it? Because to recover from our disease, we need to name it and claim it.

So it is with abuse and trauma. To fully recover, we need to name it, claim it, feel it, explore it, and tell our stories to one another. If there is any part of our history we cannot talk about, it owns us. We are the prisoner of our past. Once we can talk about it, and we do talk about it, the power shifts: we own it. We are now in charge of our own story and our own future. We are no longer prisoners of our childhood or of our wartime experience or of our trauma, whatever its cause. If we remain silent, we risk participating in the murder of our souls.

SOUL MURDER

The idea of "soul murder" is a good description of what happens to us when our abuse and trauma goes unhealed.

In 1832 in Germany, Anselm von Feuerbach published the book *Kaspar Hauser: Beispiel eines Verbrechens am Seelenleben des Menschen* (*Kaspar Hauser: The Story of a Crime against the Soul-Life of a Man*). Kaspar Hauser was an abused child. His parents kept him locked in the dark cellar of their home until he was seventeen. He had no education, even in the German language. He broke out of his confinement and wandered about the streets of Nuremberg. At first no one knew where he came from. He was taken to a hospital for the doctors to study. He could not speak, could walk only with difficulty, and acted like a two- to three-year-old child. He was found to be able to distinguish between similar colors in the dark. The doctors stated, "He may be said to be the subject of a partial 'soul murder.'" His education was very rapid. He quickly learned to speak, read, and study. However, he was emotionally unstable, and his emotional state deteriorated. He would break out of the hospital to wander the streets. In his early twenties, he was found murdered in the street. In 1974, the German film maker Werner Herzog made the first German film about the Nazi war-crimes trials, which were also held in Nuremberg. He gave his film the title *Kaspar Hauser* to symbolize the soul murder of the German people under the Nazi leadership.

In soul murder, the abusers take away a person's reason for living. Soul murder is murdering the love within a human being. Soul murder is killing the life inside a person and leaving the body standing.

When we are still children, it is can be too terrifying to tell the truth, or it may not be safe to tell the truth, so we engage in denial and repression to get by. We decide the abuse might have been our fault, or that it might have not been that bad, or that the abuser had a hard life and we can't blame them. The results are that we get shame about causing it, or being "dirty" or "bad."

A great deal more could be written about the consequences of abuse, but the focus of this chapter is healing.

STARTING ON THE PATH TO SPIRITUAL RECOVERY

The first thing needed for healing from abuse and trauma is a decision to go to any lengths to do it. This is the same as alcoholism recovery. A lot of healing involves voluntarily choosing to do things that hurt. We will need to trust God, trust ourselves, and trust our recovering friends. Many of us will need to trust a therapist as well for the complex and messy parts of this recovery.

Having decided to heal, we need a commitment to the truth, beginning with the willingness to know and speak the whole truth about our lives and our experiences. We will need to tell our story, exactly as it happened, without polite fiction or euphemisms, several times, until the story loses its power to hurt us.

I had a barrier to telling the truth. I had no idea what was true. All I knew at the outset of my healing was that I wanted to kill myself. I didn't even know why. Looking back, I know that God led me to the right psychiatrist, but neither of us knew my history. It took us two and a half years to piece together the clues from my mind and reassemble my past into its actual story. That process was extremely emotionally painful. I would schedule the psychiatrist appointment in the afternoon and a Twelve Step meeting for Adult Children of Alcoholics for that evening. In the psychiatrist's office, I opened up the pain, and then in the evening meeting, I shed some of it.

Once I visited an alcohol treatment program called Maryville. It had a Catholic heritage and lots of statues and scripture verses. One sign had a scripture verse, followed by another verse that wasn't from the Bible: "The Truth shall make you free. But first, it shall make you miserable." That statement meant a lot to me as I went through the therapy process.

None of my friends could bear to hear my story, and my wife couldn't bear it either. I recruited people to hear twenty-minute excerpts. I discovered that a number of people who cared about me could manage twenty minutes' worth. After that, they were worn out. I took what I could get. It helped.

I prayed, in a way. A lot of my prayers to God were in the form of bitter complaint. I didn't expect God to do anything. I didn't expect God to give me a different past, but I wanted God to hear me—and God did.

My abuse memories came back to me in two batches. The original set was all about beatings. Then, after a year's respite, I began to remember sexual abuse. Even though I had moved twice, for a total of twenty-two hundred miles, and he had moved once, I still ended up within ten miles of that same psychiatrist, and I went back to him. I was still practicing denial in the form of minimization when he used the word "torture" to describe what was done to me. Immediately, I was filled with rage at this kindly doctor. How dare he use that word! I thought fast, seeking the truth. I knew I had this huge wave of anger because he was telling the truth and I wanted to keep it out of my mind. Here he was, letting a whole wave of pain back into my mind. Our contract was healing and truth, and I needed to stand by the deal I had made, but I was furious! I didn't let it show.

We need to commit to ourselves, to trust God and the process of healing. We need to follow the path of truth, especially when it is painful, and trust that it will lead to freedom. The A.A.'s Big Book holds out this promise:

The great fact is just this, and nothing less: That we have had deep and effective spiritual experiences which have revolutionized our whole attitude toward life, toward our fellows, and toward God's universe. (p. 25)

My abuse and my torture ran deep. I needed to know that great fact, and nothing less. Since then I have had a deep and effective spiritual experience, which has revolutionized my whole attitude toward life, toward my fellows, and toward God's universe.

ACCEPTING GOD'S HELP

As survivors of abuse or trauma, what we believe about God will determine how well we can have spiritual recovery. The first question is whether God is our friend or our enemy. I do not believe that God caused my abuse. For a time I experienced distress because of the thought that God failed to prevent my abuse. Then I learned acceptance of life on life's terms. Even if we have acceptance, we need to examine where God stands amid the wreckage of abuse.

I approach this from the point of view of Christianity because I am a Christian. However, I don't know of any religion that accepts or justifies child abuse. No religion portrays God as approving of abuse or approving of the hatred that leads to wars. Many religions have an exception for "just" wars in defense of one's people, but no religion teaches that God endorses the suffering that comes with war.

Many abuse survivors have been injured a second time by a misunderstanding of Christianity. Well-meaning Christians have chosen to focus on Jesus Christ as judge of our sins, instead of doing a close and careful reading of the Gospels. Although one can find Bible passages that speak of God's judgment, they are relatively few. In the four Gospels of the New Testament, story after story portrays the extraordinary compassion of Christ. Especially in Luke's Gospel, many of the stories end with the phrase, "and he had compassion for them, not like the scribes and the Pharisees." Part of the reason that Jesus went to the cross was so he could fully participate in all the suffering that we go through.

Jesus said, "Whatever you do to the least of these, you do it to me." That is a direct challenge to all of us about how we treat people. If anyone abuses a child, it is the same as abusing Jesus. He has compassion for us and is not sitting there keeping score on the correctness of our responses to our abuse.

Sadly, too many people over the years have been like the scribes and Pharisees, judging the correctness of the abuse survivors' responses to their experiences. Some of our judges are religious figures who demand that we forgive our abusers long before our abusers are even called to accountability. Some of our judges are therapists or friends who have preconceived notions of the correct way for us to recover. I have known several women who were "fired" by their therapists because they would not confront their fathers about their child abuse. The therapist was being an imperialist, attempting to dominate the patient just as much as the original abuser did.

I have continued to see my original psychiatrist from 1985 every three months, even though I moved away, because of the depth of his understanding and compassion, as well as his extraordinary skills at traditional psychoanalysis. I can go and talk about anything at all for fifty minutes, and then he will reveal what I really meant to say all along.

When I moved to Minnesota, I tried adding a local therapist on a weekly basis to help with PTSD symptoms. I thought we were doing well until we bumped into her agenda for me. After I had developed some attachment to her, I was abruptly fired from therapy because I was unwilling to give up my support of the death penalty for murderers who sexually abused children and then killed them. She said I would be unable to make progress in therapy unless I could give up my support of the death penalty and that there was no point in going on, so we were done.

As we seek to provide healing and care for each other, we need to receive each other with compassion and not insist on the "right" way for the survivor to behave or recover. Outside of Christianity, my favorite spiritual figure is from Buddhism—Kwan Yin (or Quan Yin), the Bodhisattva of Compassion.

Here is where meditation becomes helpful. We can gain some peace by meditating on our relationship with the compassionate face of God. It could be Michelangelo's *The Pieta* or Buddhism's Quan Yin or the person of Jesus Christ or a just a sense that the universe is loving. We can meditate on a compassionate Higher Power enfolding us and comforting us.

EMPOWERMENT

We empower ourselves when we make a deliberate choice to accept that our Higher Power is on our side. We claim our place as children of God, and we claim our truth. We accept even our own self-doubt. Many of us who were abused have confusing or incomplete memories. We simply accept that our memories are confusing or incomplete. We may not know precisely what happened, but we can still know that something happened and that whatever did happen has had an effect on us. Staking our claim that we are who we are and that God is on our side gives us a secure base from which we can launch our recovery. When we do this, the rest of the Big Book quote from page 25 will come true:

The central fact of our lives today is the absolute certainty that our Creator has entered into our hearts and lives in a way which is indeed miraculous. He has commenced to accomplish those things for us which we could never do by ourselves.

GOALS FOR RECOVERY FROM ABUSE AND TRAUMA

I like the set of goals adopted by the program for survivors of torture at Bellevue Hospital in New York City. Their goals are that the survivor of torture would move from a sense of unpredictable danger to reliable safety, from a sense of dissociated trauma to reliable memory, and from stigmatized isolation to restored social connection.

We do this by ending all abusive relationships and forming friendships with nonabusive human beings. We do this by seeking, knowing, and telling the truth, over and over. We do this by welcoming a loving relationship with a Higher Power and with life itself.

We can achieve these goals by taking specific actions.

SETTING BOUNDARIES

The first boundary we set is to define ourselves as abuse or trauma survivors and claim our right to recovery. We claim the right to say no to other people without feeling guilty. We state to all that we will not tolerate any abuse. We have a right to privacy. We have a right to share only what we wish from our stories. We have a right to expect that our friendships will be mutual.

It took a long time for me to realize that if someone is unhappy with me, it doesn't automatically mean I am wrong. If people are unhappy with me, it is a cue to reevaluate my behavior, but I am here to do God's will in my life, so I should think in terms of what God wants me to do. I don't put all my decisions up for a vote.

I heard a useful phrase at a meeting, "I've got to stop auctioning myself off to the low bidder." As an abused child, I learned to pay careful attention to the angriest person in my environment, because that was the one who was most likely to abuse me. That made sense, and it probably helped me avoid a lot of beatings. That intense focus on people who don't like me isn't so helpful today. I need to focus on what God wants me to do, not on what my harshest critic wants me to do.

BREAKING THE "NO TALK" RULE

We need to break the "no talk" rule. As children we may have heard, "If you don't have something nice to say, don't say anything at all." Also, the experience of childhood abuse naturally leads to wordlessness. The child who is being abused has no words to describe his or her experience.

Until the last few years, children were not given any words with which they could talk about abuse. The wordlessness of their experience carried over to the adult experience of survivors who were in their therapists' offices, unable to express why they were so depressed. In recent years, children at least are being taught the phrase "bad touch" so they will have some words to describe their experiences.

SHARING WITH OTHER SURVIVORS

We need to connect with other survivors and share our experience, strength, and hope. Alcoholics could not recover until they came together as groups using the Twelve Steps. Now, in major cities at least, there are Twelve Step groups for incest survivors. My experience is that the quality of these groups varies, but they are at least worth checking out. If there isn't a suitable Twelve Step group focusing on abuse survivors, we can inquire within our existing Twelve Step group and ask to talk with abuse survivors privately or in informal small groups.

REMEMBERING AND RECLAIMING THE PAST

We may need time for extended remembrance and mourning for our lives. We may have lost much over many years. We can write grief letters to ourselves or to an earlier version of ourselves at the age when we were abused. We can do letters to or from our childhood selves, telling ourselves how it really was and comforting ourselves. We can let ourselves be the children today that we once were too afraid to be.

One rainy day, I was driving down Broadway in Everett, Massachusetts, and saw an object in the middle of the road that looked somewhat like a towel. Traffic was slow. As I got closer, I realized it was a badly worn stuffed animal that had been run over quite a few times. I had a strong emotional reaction. I wanted to rescue it. I censored those feelings and made myself drive by. I thought, *Don't be ridiculous. It's just a torn-up stuffed animal. It doesn't have any feelings. It doesn't need rescuing. Forget about it.* Other things happened on that drive, and I did forget.

Hours later I was driving home, and it was still there. This time I felt horrible! I swerved to the side of the road, jumped out into the rain, ran into traffic, and grabbed it. I had the filthy outer cover of a teddy bear. After I sent it through the laundry several times, I had a teddy bear cover with a gaping hole in the back and no stuffing. I called the friend from New Hampshire who had taken me on the "mystery adventure." She agreed to try to help the teddy bear. She got stuffing and added cloth where the original had been ripped away. I named him "Survivor Bear" and he became my toy.

I never had a stuffed animal as a child. My older sister had one—a stuffed dog—but our mom destroyed it in a rage. Because I saw what happened to my sister's stuffed dog, I never tried to get one. So, as an adult, I put aside my feelings of foolishness and immaturity and rescued "Survivor Bear."

ALLOWING ANGRY FEELINGS

We need to be able to be angry without doing any harm. It is helpful to become angry with our abusers in a direct, clear, and focused way. When we can be angry and feel angry, it does not leak out of us sideways and injure people who do not deserve our anger. The anger may come out well enough if we tell our story in depth, with emotion. We may also benefit from an "anger list," which is a list of specific things or events we are angry about. We may also do an anger letter to our abuser, which may or may not be appropriate to send but which should be written with complete clarity. Angry, but harmless, actions can help. Some people chop wood or beat a sofa with a tennis racquet.

Because I have held firearms licenses for many years, I have taken friends who are abuse survivors to firing ranges.

They write whatever they want on paper targets, then shoot at them. I've found it best to take two guns and rotate them because some of my friends have been so angry that they fire so fast and so long the gun barrels might overheat. Afterward, they reported feeling a lot better. It helped me release anger, too. My wife of thirty-seven years has seen me very angry. She tells me she appreciates the fact that I don't take my anger out on her.

REBELLING AGAINST SHAME

We need to challenge any sense of shame we have from our abuse. We need to accept that our shame is not about who we are but about how we were treated. We are bearing the shame that belongs to someone else. The truth is that survivors of abuse should not hide. Perpetrators of abuse should hide. We are sometimes ashamed of the symptoms of abuse and trauma. We take the symptoms and use them to call ourselves "sick." Abuse and trauma can be associated with a whole range of psychological and social problems: depression, isolation, difficulty making friends, alcoholism, sexual maladjustment, an exaggerated startle reflex, and chronic fear, among many other things. None of these signs of damage are actually things to be ashamed of.

One day as I was talking with my psychiatrist in the course of recovering from the torture, I referred to myself as "sick." He looked startled and said, "You're not sick, you're injured." That shift in point of view made a lot of difference. It was not that I was defective, it was that I had suffered a traumatic injury that had damaged me. It was not my fault. (I never even considered that a sickness might not be my fault, either.) We need to rebel against a sense of shame.

Confronting our abusers may or may not be a worthwhile goal. Are they still alive? Will confronting them put us at risk of new trauma? Are we confronting them to clear the air and to own our own truth, or are we confronting them with a covert hope that they will then apologize to us and make it all better? (If the latter, we may be setting ourselves up for revictimization.) This is an individual choice that depends on the situation. It should be made together with supportive friends and with the benefit of prayer and meditation so we can know our Higher Power's will for our lives.

RECLAIMING PLAY AND INNOCENCE

We need to rediscover play and innocence. We need the ability to touch others and to be touched in a kindly way. Priscilla had correctly intuited that she should never touch my face, because I had been hit in the face so many times and had experienced major facial injuries. She probably saw me flinch when she got near. Then one night, she rolled over in her sleep, and her elbow whapped me hard in the face. In an instant, I sat bolt upright. I grabbed her by the neck and was about to punch her when I caught myself and stopped. This badly frightened both of us.

The next evening we sat on a sofa and I practiced letting her touch my face, very gently. It was terrible. I just wanted to hit her—badly. I recognized the desire as a legacy of my abuse, but my wiring was very strong. I suffered through the touching until I was confident we could have another accident like the one the night before without my automatically fighting with her. Most people's bad reactions aren't that bad, but even a slight cringe or pulling away can hurt our relationships, and we may need to practice with those we love to overcome the years of physical programming that came from our abuse. Today I have no hesitation to embrace her or to be embraced in any way.

A FINAL WORD ON FORGIVENESS

I don't make forgiveness a goal, because I see it as a gift from God, not something we can achieve on our own. We cannot set a goal and a timeline for something only God can give to us. However, we can *want* to forgive, and we can *hope* to experience forgiveness.

In time, I had released my abusers to the care of the universe. How it happened was that I was struggling with my sense of duty to forgive them and my inability to forgive them. If I had a duty to do something I couldn't do, then I was stuck. Finally, I said to God: "Look, I resign from the whole forgiveness business. I'm going to subcontract the whole forgiveness business to you because I can't do it and because you're God, not me. So you do it. Forgive them, don't forgive them. Your choice. Let them into heaven, send them to hell. Send them to heck if there is one. I resign as God. It's entirely up to you. I'm letting go of the whole thing."

To my surprise, that actually worked. I just said it because I was frustrated and stuck. I couldn't decide how I was supposed to reconcile my feelings of hurt and anger with a socially imposed mandate to forgive them. Then I remembered: if I have turned my will and my life over to God's care, I can also turn each unsolvable problem over to God's care. Turning the mess over to God allowed me to release my abusers. Several years later I noticed that I had forgiven them.

COMPLETE RESTORATION

Marie Fortune, a clergywoman who worked with abuse survivors in Washington state and specialized in working with survivors of clergy abuse, made a list of elements that could make things right in the lives of survivors. They were:

1. Truth telling
2. Acknowledgment
3. Compassion
4. Protecting the vulnerable
5. Call to accountability
6. Making restitution
7. Vindication and setting free

Rev. Fortune was referring to a social system that wanted to do the right thing. We may or may not have the cooperation of those around us, but the elements of healing are still important. It is more common than not that abusers do not accept responsibility for the abuse and will not make amends. What then? We can still look to have these elements of healing fulfilled by God and by our fellow human beings in our Twelve Step programs.

Our truth telling needs to be matched with compassionate listeners who will acknowledge our stories, and we need to tell our stories directly to God, whose compassion is big enough to absorb all of our pain and suffering.

We survivors need to examine our current living situation and our current relationships for signs that we are vulnerable to maltreatment in the present. Are we listening to the language of hostility and contempt in any of our relationships? Are we dependent on people who don't like us? Then it may be time for structural change, including ending relationships that are hostile, exploitive, or unkind.

We need to call the sources of our abuse or trauma to accountability by naming them in public and naming their behavior. We may not get restitution from the perpetrators of abuse, but we may award ourselves some restitution of our own according to what is financially possible, from a comforting blanket to a warm and safe home.

We need to be vindicated and set free by our God and our community. Many of the soldiers traumatized during the Vietnam era had their traumatic wounds deepened because their home community, America, refused to even look at them when they came home. In large parts of America, their service went unrecognized and their trauma went unacknowledged. A majority of the American people now recognize that our behavior back then was wrong, and we are respecting today's veterans. All survivors of trauma deserve a "welcome home" from their community.

When our stories are told and believed, when we are received with compassion by God and our fellows, and when the community of which we are a part upholds us and upholds the justice of our cause, then we can be free.

CHAPTER 6:

LOVE AND ROMANCE

―――

WHY DO ALCOHOLICS/ADDICTS HAVE SUCH TROUBLE WITH LOVE/ROMANCE?

Selfishness, self-centeredness! That, we think, is the root of our troubles. Driven by a hundred forms of fear, self-delusion, self-seeking, and self-pity, we step on the toes of our fellows, and they retaliate. (Alcoholics Anonymous, p. 61)

It is normal to want a loving, intimate relationship with another human being, but it is somehow hard to get. The obvious barrier to intimacy, closeness, and trust is selfishness, but hidden behind those is fear. With love comes the inevitable certainty of loss. It is not a risk of loss, it is a certainty of loss. Until we can face the certainty of loss, and the pain and grief that will come with loss, we won't be able to let go of our fears and fully love.

Fear of loss causes us to hold back from fully committing to love. I have been married to Priscilla for thirty-seven years, and for most of that time, I did not fully commit to her—I held back a portion of myself. I finally realized I was holding back a part of myself so that if I lost her, there would be a part of me that hadn't been put out there, a part of me that wasn't at risk. I could use this part that had never been at risk to rescue the rest of me from total loss. It seemed like safety at the time.

But loss is certain. At this writing, I am sixty-four. I can try telling myself that I am not old, but the argument is shaky. Priscilla is seventy-four. She is definitely getting old. One of us will die first. One of us will be devastated by that death. A big loss is a certainty.

I paid a price for my decision to hold part of myself in reserve. I never felt completely "there" with Priscilla. I would include her and our marriage in my prayers. I would ask God to take care of me, of her, and of us. In the meditation that followed, I kept hearing God ask, "If not now, when?" That question, which kept coming up in meditation, didn't come with an explanation. I came to realize it meant that if I would not commit to loving her fully now, when would I ever do it?

The Narcotics Anonymous basic text tells us in the chapter "Recovery and Relapse" that we should do our program without reservations and without loopholes, because keeping reservations or loopholes in our lives leads to relapse. A.A. tells us that "half-measures availed us nothing." They were writing about getting sober. Half-measures can get us half a relationship, but I wanted the whole thing. I had to let go of my reservations to get everything I could out of being married.

LOVING SOMEONE OR WANTING THEM

Love is an emotion, but it is also a way of life. When we love someone, we want every good thing for them. We orient our thoughts, our feelings, and our actions toward seeking every possible benefit in life for them. We think about little things and large things that would make them happy. We encourage them to pursue their life goals, even if it means compromising our own. We provide for their physical security, their financial security, and their emotional security by helping them have a safe home and be truly emotionally safe in our company.

On the other hand, when we *want* someone, we want them for ourselves. We notice every good thing about them, but we want all those good things for ourselves. We orient our thoughts, our feelings, and our actions toward gaining every possible benefit in life out of our relationship with them. We make an early sexual connection because it has a powerful emotional pull that makes us hard to leave, and we focus our behaviors on making the other person want us.

Love is rooted in self-giving. Wanting is rooted in self-centeredness. Both emotions are strong, but loving frees the other person, while wanting attempts to bind them.

Loving someone is rooted in appreciation for another person the way he or she actually is. Love does not seek to change the other person. Wanting is based on needing the other person to fit some preexisting role we desire to have filled. Wanting accepts the other person only briefly before attempting to change him or her into the person we believe we need. Loving focuses on changing ourselves; wanting focuses on changing the other person.

Love is willing to allow intimacy to grow slowly and naturally over time. Because wanting is based on fear of loss, wanting pushes for too much intimacy too fast, which can result in a pattern of approach and avoidance. In this pattern, we try to get too close too fast, and then the intense feelings frighten us off. We may have an argument and pull back to the edge of splitting up. Then our attraction pulls us back together until it is way too close for comfort, then we argue and split up, and the pattern repeats. The strong urge for intimacy and the fear of intimacy collide.

Because wanting is based on fear of loss, wanting is often accompanied by demands for love and attention, to "prove" one's love. In wanting, we demand demonstrations of love. In loving, we show love based on our loving hearts. Wanting is often upset by any show of autonomy in the other, due to a fear of losing the other person, who the wanting heart believes has been newly "acquired." A loving person knows we don't own each other and is willing to trust the other person, even when the other person has a life outside of the relationship. The loving person parts easily at times of routine separation. The wanting person avoids any separation.

The key decision in any relationship is this: will I go forward based on *loving* the other person or on *wanting* the other person? They may feel alike, but the behaviors are entirely different.

The trouble is, we may not know there is any difference between loving and wanting. We may not notice the difference because we aren't thinking about our behavior at all. Instead, we are caught up in feelings of romance.

ROMANCE

Romance is an intense, short-lived emotion of attraction to an idealized version of another person. In romance, we don't see the person as he or she *is* but as we *want* him or her to be—the person of our dreams, the fulfillment of all our wishes and desires. We fall in love not with the real person but with our fantasy of who the person is, or who he or she will be after we have completed the job of perfecting him or her.

Romance is a combination of wanting and the imagined fulfillment of that same wanting. It is both the dream and the dream come true, all in one. A normal reaction to mutual romance is for the two people involved to merge so quickly and so totally that the resulting pileup is called a "crush." Imagining that they have both found perfect happiness, neither person has any reason to hold anything in reserve, and they move in together, merge finances, and give up careers and life choices just to be together all the time.

Romance is characterized by failing to distinguish between one person and the other. Everything one person thinks, feels, or does impacts the other person right away. There is no longer any such thing as a private life. Because of the crush, individual boundaries are weakened or gone, and increasingly both people feel the need to have the other person there and in agreement in order to feel safe or even whole.

Unfortunately, once a couple is together all the time, it is hard to maintain romantic perfection twenty-four hours a day. If it's four in the morning and neither of you can sleep and you both have the flu, it's really hard to be romantic at that moment. Being with each other all the time and thinking about each other all the time begins to reveal little flaws in the relationship. It's no longer perfect.

The couple whose relationship is based on wanting the other person to live up to the image of romantic perfection are now going to become increasingly anxious about not getting what they want.

THE BREAKDOWN OF ROMANCE

When we are afraid of losing the ideal partner we have imagined, our behavior gets controlling. We try to take care of the other person's feelings. We try to tell them how they should feel. We may give gifts and favors in order to get what we want. We may start trying to keep them from leaving us, even for a brief time. We may tell them how dependent we have become with phrases like "I can't live without you."

Because romance was never real to begin with, when we try to inhabit it and make it come true, disappointment is inevitable. There is a better way to deal with romance.

THE ENJOYMENT OF ROMANCE

Most people reading this book will have moved well past their first romance in life. There's nothing wrong with romance, as long as we know that the idealized view of the other person isn't real. If we recognize it as a very enjoyable emotional experience, but not necessarily a good planning tool, we can have fun. Being in love feels great! Enjoy it! It brings couples together and allows them to be playful and to explore their relationship without the seriousness that makes life hard.

Romance combined with love is rocket fuel for relationships. I can recognize that romance makes me more optimistic than I might otherwise be, more forgiving, more tolerant, and more hopeful in the face of setbacks—but those things are good for us as a couple. I never thought of myself as naturally romantic, but I discovered in my marriage to Priscilla that cleaning up the kitchen or taking out the trash, picking up after myself, and doing laundry turned out to be romantic. Who knew?

I have also, on some of our wedding anniversaries, written her love letters. They are not traditionally romantic in that they don't resemble the language of greeting cards, but they have spelled out in detail, at different stages of our marriage, what it is about her that made me love her. On our twenty-fifth wedding anniversary, I wrote her twenty-five short love letters, one for each year of our marriage. Each letter recalled something from that year (first, second, and so on) that represented something I loved about her. She will treasure them always and pass them down to our daughters when she dies.

SOME MORE CHARACTERISTICS OF LOVE

If we love someone, we give that person a specific commitment to nonviolence in every form: in our thoughts, our words, and our attitudes, as well as our actions. If we really love them, we should give them no reason to ever be afraid of us.

If we love someone, we are on the lookout for opportunities to reduce pain in his or her life. Put some slack in the system when the system is under stress. Take on some of their chores when they have extra work to do.

If we love someone, we are clear about what we want and we are gracious if we don't get it, don't get it all, or don't get it right away. Priscilla and I have a saying: "If you don't get what you didn't ask for, don't be sore." Enmeshed couples sometimes want the other person to be a mind reader, on the theory that "if you loved me, you would know what I wanted."

If we love someone, we offer that person the opportunity to reinvent him- or herself at different stages of life. I thought Priscilla and I were settled just fine as copastors of four rural

Methodist churches in northern New Hampshire when she decided she wanted to study feminist liberation theology for a year. That meant leaving our jobs and our home and going away for a year, with no jobs and no place to live. My first thought was how inconvenient that was for me. But we had already committed to try to help each other grow and change, so I said yes right away.

I thank God I said yes, because it led to a wonderful opportunity for me to study at Hazelden and it led me to sobriety when I met the men in treatment there. If I had been selfish and self-seeking and had talked her out of it, I could have died of my addiction during these past twenty-four years.

Then, five years later, when I had the chance to return to Hazelden as supervisor of spiritual care, Priscilla was willing to make the move to Minnesota so I could take the opportunity here. We understand that the people we married in 1976 are not the people we will always be. We've helped make each other better.

If we love someone, we give gifts without the expectation of something in return. On our first wedding anniversary, Priscilla and I gave self-serving gifts. I gave her a Mr. Coffee machine, and she gave me a full-length mirror. She doesn't drink coffee, and I never look in the mirror to see if my clothes match. We've gotten more thoughtful about our gifts. Priscilla has wanted to go to Egypt for the last twenty-five years. I always said no because of the civil unrest and attacks on tourist sites—until she stopped asking. Every year, I checked the State Department's travel warnings site, and a few years ago it cleared Egypt as safe for tourist travel. It still was not a trip I wanted. Because of traumatic brain injuries, I am very averse to bright sunlight, and Egypt has lots of it. Nonetheless, I told her of the opportunity, and she was very happy to go. I arranged a fine trip that covered many of the best ancient sites, and we went.

If we love someone, we apply Step Ten to ourselves daily, and when we are wrong in the relationship, we promptly admit it and make amends at once. Priscilla and I have argued and been angry many times over the years. We have worked hard to settle our differences the same day if we possibly can, which has made for some late nights. As a result, we actually settle issues, instead of postponing them. We argue much less than before, and I cannot actually remember the last time we were angry with each other. Perhaps she does. I don't think I'll ask.

THE TWELVE TRADITIONS, LOVE, AND ROMANCE

The Twelve Traditions of the Twelve Step programs can be applied to relationships to help us know how to express our love for one another. The traditions were written to help us have spiritually healthy groups that operate in peace and harmony with maximum effectiveness. Couples and families are small groups, and many of the Twelve Traditions can help us be loving, just as they help our Twelve Step groups be loving instead of selfish.

TRADITION ONE

Tradition One of Alcoholics Anonymous states: "Our common welfare should come first; personal recovery depends upon A.A. unity."

In a loving relationship, we can figure out that our personal happiness depends on our unity as a couple. We can decide that whatever we happen to disagree about is less important than our relationship. Our loving unity is our goal, not the short-term goal of "winning" our disagreement. One of the differences in my marriage is that I am ten and a half years younger than my wife. It also happens that, in our society, women tend to live about nine or ten years longer than men. So we looked at each other at the beginning, considered our differences in age, and said, "Meet you at the end!" (of life).

TRADITION TWO

Tradition Two states: "For our group purpose there is but one ultimate authority—a loving God as He may express Himself in our group conscience. Our leaders are but trusted servants; they do not govern."

There are two useful ideas here. The first is that we are not alone as a couple. If we have spiritual lives, then hopefully we both have a Higher Power. We do not need to agree on what that Higher Power is to have one. If the only thing we bring to a relationship is our own resources, then we have a hard time making our loving intentions come true, just as if the only thing we bring to recovery from alcoholism is our own unassisted will, we have a hard time staying sober.

Group conscience is a different kind of decision making than is normal in our society. Voting is normal, and the majority rules. Voting doesn't work in a two-person relationship, because there are too many tie votes. Trading one thing for another works, but there are some things we are unwilling to trade. In group conscience, people in a Twelve Step group carefully consider a question, with a desire to discern God's will for the group. They will often continue to consider the question over the course of several weeks, giving extra time and attention to minority opinions, until it becomes clear to the informed conscience of the group what they should do.

Couples can do that. We can move away from the dynamic of "If you win, then I lose" and consider together which outcome is likely to leave our collective conscience at peace, which outcome can leave us content that we have done what God wants us to do in this situation. If that isn't clear, perhaps we need more time and the willingness to pray for knowledge of the next right thing to do.

The second part of this tradition tells us about a special type of leadership: leadership in service, not leadership in governance. Have we ever tried to govern our partner in a relationship? How did it go? If we try to govern them, then they are in a perfect position to rebel against us and conflict is all ready to go. If we are parents, how about trying to govern teenagers? That's also a lost cause.

I was as unprepared to be a father as I was to be a husband. I decided to try to be of service to my preteen daughters. I knew that when they reached eighteen, they were free to leave our home and, say, hitchhike to Arizona if they wanted to. So I decided to try to serve them by teaching them life skills so they could be competent adults. I wanted them to be able to balance a checkbook, apply for a job, and make their way in the adult world. I hoped that they would accept the family offer to go to college, but if they headed out on their own at eighteen, I wanted them to be able to do it.

If I had tried to govern Priscilla, I don't think we would have stayed together. She is, as she has expressed it, "The only radical feminist I know who is still married." By loving her without trying to change her, we've ended up in a loving relationship.

TRADITION THREE

Tradition Three states: "The only requirement for A.A. membership is a desire to stop drinking." The beauty of this tradition in A.A. is that once we express a desire to stop drinking, we're in. There are no periodic requalification tests. We can relax, knowing that any mistakes we make will not sever our ties to the fellowship.

To apply this tradition to relationships, we could say that the only requirement for membership in this relationship is the desire to be in it. That's it. We don't have to have the same political views. We don't have to like the same people, laugh at the same television shows, have the same religion, or agree on much at all except that we want to love and care for each other. Sometimes when I have been really angry over a disagreement, I have blurted out, "F--- this, I love you anyhow!" This would be totally out of context, and sometimes it makes her laugh.

TRADITION FOUR

Tradition Four states: "Each group should be autonomous except in matters affecting other groups or A.A. as a whole." Part of the vitality of A.A. is that there is no central office that reins in groups that get out of line. This frees groups to be creative about how they carry a message of hope to the alcoholic who still suffers. There are groups that hold motorcycle rallies, groups that hold sunrise meetings on the beach, and groups that carry the message into state prisons, with no one there to regulate them and make them careful.

In loving relationships, each person should be autonomous unless it would damage the couple or the family as a whole. Priscilla likes her autonomy to go off and do things that interest her and don't interest me. She has gone on two Asian trips to the Philippines and Thailand with a feminist group to explore and publicize the sex trafficking of women. Recently, she has been involved with a nonprofit group called Mano a Mano, which builds and operates medical clinics in poor rural mountain towns in Bolivia. In the winter of 2012, at the age of seventy-three, she was off to the mountains of Bolivia with a Mano a Mano group to open a new clinic. Each summer, she is away for two to three weeks at the Adlerian Psychotherapy International Summer School, and in the summer of 2012, she's in Vilnius, Lithuania. While she is away in the summer, I take a long weekend and play tour guide for Minnesota friends who have never been to my home town of New York City. If our relationship was rooted in fear of abandonment, we'd never let each other out of our sight. Love and respect for autonomy allow us to part with confidence and reunite with joy.

TRADITION FIVE

Tradition Five states: "Each group has but one primary purpose—to carry the message to the alcoholic who still suffers." This is called A.A.'s singleness of purpose. By focusing on one thing, it accomplishes it. If it had many purposes, it would be at risk of failing to accomplish any of them.

We can decide that each of us in a relationship has but one primary purpose—to create a relationship of love and trust for both people. We are not planning to be a "power" couple or a "hot" couple or a "prominent" couple or a "stylish" couple—even though any of those things could happen.

Our decision was tested in 2005, when I had a dangerous brain virus called Ramsey-Hunt. I went into a coma, and when I came out, I could not think at all, just perceive. Then I began to have thoughts that consisted of one word only, and I could not communicate. Then I got thoughts that had a couple of words, and I could speak a little bit. Then I went home from the hospital.

I could not read. I had no emotions at all. I could think and speak only with difficulty. I don't really know what I was like, because my thinking at the time was very limited. There was no assurance that I would get better. I was fifty-three years old.

Priscilla was faced with the prospect that she might have to live with me that way: a husband who could only say a few words at a time and who had no emotions. She has since told me that she realized in church that although she "had fallen in love with my brilliant mind," she had come to appreciate even more my human goodness, and that was still there.

TRADITION SIX

Tradition Six states: "An A.A. group ought never endorse, finance or lend the A.A. name to any related facility or outside enterprise, lest problems of money, property and prestige divert us from our primary purpose." A.A. has a firm rule against outside affiliations. This simple, rigid rule protects A.A. from being lured into believing that a money issue is more important than recovery, or believing more in a piece of property than in recovery, or being swayed by public praise or prestige.

Each of us as an individual has lots of outside affiliations. We have jobs, religions, political parties, and friendship groups. We may already own property that we are obliged to look after. We all have money needs. We cannot meet our personal financial needs by passing a basket, as A.A. does. We can, however, be careful to prevent any of these outside affiliations from getting in the way of our primary purpose as a couple, which is to have a relationship of love and trust.

If we are overcommitted to work, we will make the mistake of giving our best at the workplace and leaving leftovers for our relationship. If we draw our primary identity from our job titles, then we are offering just a small piece of our hearts to our partners. If we give ourselves completely to a cause, we may leave our partners wondering how we can care so much about "people" and so little about them. I have a slogan: "In order to retain the title, a lover must keep on loving."

Tradition Six tells us that our outside affiliations should be left there: outside.

TRADITION SEVEN

Tradition Seven states: "Every A.A. group ought to be fully self-supporting, declining outside contributions." This tradition has given A.A. durability. By not taking federal funds, A.A. is immune to federal budget cuts. In about 1978, the Veterans Administration shut down a great residential alcoholism-treatment program at the VA hospital in White River Junction, Vermont. I went to an event that was held to say good-bye. I thought there might be some negativity about the government's decision, but there wasn't. People were grateful for all that had happened there, they said good-bye to their friends who were being laid off, and they commented on the wisdom of A.A. in not taking any federal money. People said they were so glad that A.A. could never be shut down by taking away its money. It was not dependent on the government, on United Way, or on anyone. It was self-supporting by its own contributions.

The financial independence that gives A.A. its freedom gives couples their freedom, too. That may mean we both work or both work long hours. That may mean we don't buy on credit, beyond a home and a car. I have known couples who spent many years suppressing what they really thought and wanted because they were awaiting an inheritance that might not come, and then it didn't come and they were crushed. I have known couples who accepted not being happy in the present because their hope was to win the lottery someday.

My slogan is: "If your outgo exceeds your income, then your upkeep becomes your downfall." Too many couples live by borrowing and never discuss what is happening to them.

If you are not self-supporting and living within your income now as a couple, become honest and loving with each other. Share information with each other without engaging in shame or blame. This calls for disciplined love. Clear a table. Put every financial document on it. Add up what you owe and make a plan, without one word of blame or shame. As the Big Book puts it, "Acceptance is the answer to *all* my problems today" (p. 417). Decide that love and trust will lead you to the right answers together.

Once the finances are in order, just check in once in a while to let each other know that you are self-supporting and living within your income and that your long-term plans—for a home, for retirement—are under way. This will add to the sense of security and trust that gives love an extra dimension.

TRADITIONS EIGHT AND NINE

Traditions Eight and Nine have to do with the structure of A.A. and do not seem to have direct applicability to couples.

TRADITION TEN

Tradition Ten states: "Alcoholics Anonymous has no opinion on outside issues; hence the A.A. name ought never be drawn into public controversy." Again, A.A. has taken a rigid position for the protection of the groups.

Each person in a couple can have any number of opinions on outside issues, but it is useful to be able to downgrade our emotional attachment to those positions below the level of our emotional attachment to the person we love. Issues come and go. I don't want my primary relationship to come and go. We need to decide that outside issues are less important than our primary relationship of love and trust.

I've stated that I didn't have useful role models at home when I was growing up. However, I did have some useful role models on the job when I held a variety of blue-collar jobs between ages sixteen and twenty-seven. Some of those men seemed happy in their marriages. One of their sayings was, "Never s--- where you eat." It was inelegant, but I got the point. It meant, "Don't make trouble at home."

I have had a persistent problem of being over impressed with my brilliance, and so I have been ready to argue a great many issues. Only slowly did I realize that people were not usually pleased when I beat them in an argument. Gradually, I came to adopt the slogan "I'd rather be useful than right." Being right often damaged my relationships. Being useful helped. I gradually figured that out.

In my marriage now, Priscilla and I often have opposite opinions, but we've made it part of what we love about each other. On election day, our votes cancel each other's out about half the time, but we both go and vote. I even get the *Saint Paul Pioneer Press* candidate's page and point out to Priscilla why she would want to vote for the candidates she often ends up supporting. I often vote against them for the same reasons. Our love and trust is more important than the election, and we are only two votes out of thousands.

TRADITION ELEVEN

Tradition Eleven is about maintaining personal anonymity in the programs. There is no need to do that in a relationship. We don't keep it a secret that we are in love. We do, however, maintain privacy for our partner. We simply do not tell anything about the other unless we are confident that he or she is willing to have it told. We do this to maintain the atmosphere of love and trust.

TRADITION TWELVE

Tradition Twelve states: "Anonymity is the spiritual foundation of all our Traditions, ever reminding us to place principles before personalities."

Anonymity keeps us from thinking we are a big deal. Anonymity keeps us from thinking that our thoughts and feelings matter more than the thoughts and feelings of our partners. When I was still drinking, my attitude was "I want WHAT I want, WHEN I want it. WHAT I want is MORE, and WHEN I want it is NOW!" When I began to change, and think about other people, I would joke, "I may not be much, but I'm all I think about." It might sound humble, but it wasn't.

This tradition has been more helpful to me than any other, because it gives me a constant, gentle redirection of my thoughts and attitudes. It gives me a nudge from selfishness to spirituality. It reminds me that Priscilla is not just "my wife" or an adjunct to me but a whole and distinct person, a child of God, who has chosen to make a commitment to me, and that I have the privilege of making a commitment to her. These traditions and our Higher Power give us the ability to make those commitments come true.

LOVE, ROMANCE, AND SEXUALITY

The discussion of sexuality in loving relationships comes last because many couples make the mistake of putting it first. It is, unfortunately, a common practice of people who want to be in an exclusive relationship to first have sex, and then if the sex is any good, they try to find out who the other person is.

That practice is based on the theory that sex is a lot of fun and as emotionally harmless as bowling. Here there is often a gender difference. Many men can have sex without an emotional attachment. Far fewer women can have sex without an emotional attachment. In couples who have sex within the first months of a relationship, an emotional imbalance is set in motion, with a big opportunity for hurt feelings. An emotional attraction that would honestly be expressed as "I want sex" is verbalized as "I love you" and is often believed. Actually, "I love you" can merely mean "I believe in saying 'I love you.'" When I lecture on early sobriety, to male and female patients separately, I recommend to both groups that they follow a common A.A. and N.A. suggestion: refrain from any new sexual relationship for the first year of sobriety. The programs make this recommendation because they have become aware of how the emotional pain of breakups after hookups can cause relapse. In my lectures, I include this statement: "Remember: women can fake orgasms; men can fake love." Usually, the men don't laugh, but the women do—they know.

The truth is that sex can't be better than the relationship it is part of. When we shoot for that great sexual high without love, we usually end up using drugs to try to get it. They might be "safe" drugs like Viagra or "dangerous" drugs like amyl nitrate, but somehow, just the other person isn't enough to meet our sexual desires if we separate sex from love.

A relationship of love, trust, safety, and comfort allows human sexuality to flow naturally. Both Priscilla and I are damaged in the area of sexuality: I from being abused by an uncle and cousin when I was ten and eleven years old, she from being abused by her first husband when she was a young woman. Somehow, with love, great caution, and sensitivity to each other, we are able to have fully satisfying sexual experiences with each other at the ages of sixty-four and seventy-four. If popular humor is to be believed, many couples our age who have been married thirty-seven years no longer have a sexual relationship at all.

There's also romance for us. We have candlelight dinners at home most evenings, and we don't answer the phone during dinner. We hold hands when we walk together. We talk to each other in restaurants, instead of peering into electronic devices. We have our own secret language, with shorthand words and sounds that express feelings. I always say "I love you" before leaving home. I know that someday one of us will die. I want to be sure, every day, that if I don't come back, the last thing I ever said to her was, "I love you."

If we think that love is only a feeling, we may end up wondering where our love has gone. Once we know that love is a behavior, as well as a feeling, we know how to get more love in our lives, by behaving in a loving way.

CHAPTER 7:

HOPE

Hope is absolutely necessary for recovery, and for happiness. We cannot be happy all the time, but we can have hope all the time. The disease of addiction thrives on hopelessness. It tells us to give up our efforts, and revert to drinking and drugging. I need to renew my hope every day: Hope that God, my sober friends, and this program will work for me again today, as it has for twenty-four years.

HOPE VERSUS FEAR IN RECOVERY

Hope works better than fear as a motivator for recovery. This might seem obvious to recovering people, but "normal" people—or "earth people," as I refer to them—often try to use fear as a motivator. It just doesn't work. Those of my age may remember a TV show called *Scared Straight*, in which impressionable teenagers were taken into a state prison where intimidating lifers growled at them: "Don't use drugs or you'll end up here!" It had no impact on drug use. Then there was Nancy Reagan's "Just Say No to Drugs" program. "Just Say No to Drugs" was printed on milk cartons. It turns out that addicts don't drink a lot of milk, and

"Just Say No" works until we say, "Just Say Yes," and then it's over.

Fear doesn't have the same impact on addicts as is does on nonaddicts. If we told the average heroin addict, "If you use heroin one more time, we're going to cut your legs off with a rusty chain saw," their reaction would probably be, "I've got to get really high—that's going to hurt!" We just don't change our behavior out of fear, but we will change if we gain hope.

We often leave treatment, or our first ninety days of meetings, with a lot of hope. It is sometimes dismissed as a "pink cloud," but it is real. Then life's hardships cause the hope to fade. There comes a time, sometimes six months to two years into recovery, when we look around us and ask, "I stopped drinking for *this*?" No. We didn't quit drinking and drugging just to not drink and not take drugs. There's a whole lot more to recovery than just not using chemicals. Nobody says, "Hey! It's Friday night. Let's go out and not drink!" Just not drinking and just not drugging is depressing, because the focus is on what we can't have rather than what we can have.

We may have come into treatment for a cocaine or heroin problem, and while we are there our counselor suggests that we abstain from all mood-altering chemicals, including alcohol. We ask, "You mean, I can NEVER have a drink AGAIN?" The counselor backtracks and says we shouldn't think about it as never again; we should think about it as not taking a drink one day at a time. We suspect there is a trick going on here. If we don't take a drink one day at a time for long enough, it adds up to forever. Then we get upset.

If we take an alcoholic and all we do for that alcoholic is remove the alcohol from the alcohol-ic, then what we have left is an "ic." The native sound of the "ic" is whining, and whining is simply anger coming through a hole that is too small. We just hate it when our chemicals are taken away and nothing is given back.

Because I have been working with alcoholics and addicts for thirty-seven years, I get to think about and talk about the meaning and purpose of life. This is important, because the human being is the only mammal that will seek to destroy itself if it suspects that its life has no meaning. Addiction increases the sense that our lives have no meaning.

In addiction, as we get sicker, we can come to a state of mind, emotion, and spirit I call "extreme indifference." In my home state of New York, we are charged with manslaughter if we take an action that causes someone's death unintentionally but through our reckless actions and with, the law says, "extreme indifference" as to whether the person lived or died—and they died. In addiction, we sometimes do that to ourselves.

Sometimes an addict or alcoholic turns up dead of an overdose, and there's no suicide note. The question is, was it an accident or a suicide? The truth is, it was somewhere in between. The dead addict wasn't trying to become dead; he or she was trying to become numb, but the dosage required to become numb was close to the dosage required to become dead. They knew it was unsafe. They knew it could kill them, but the addiction was just too strong, so they acted recklessly and with extreme indifference as to whether they lived or died, and they died.

So if this powerful desire to become numb is a part of the disease, then the willingness to go ahead and feel what we feel is part of recovery. For us to go ahead and feel painful and difficult feelings when it is easier to seek numbness, we have to have some hope that it will come out all right and that there will be a payoff worth the pain.

Where does this hope come from? There are four sources of hope I have found: reality, gratitude, transformation, and angels.

REALITY AS A SOURCE OF HOPE

The beginning of reality is getting the chemicals out of our brains. With drugs in our brains, we cannot know reality. We think things that are not true, and we have feelings that are not accurate.

With stimulant drugs like methamphetamine and cocaine, most of our feelings are missing—except for alert, bullet-proof, paranoid, and angry emotions, followed by "crash and burn." With opiates, our feelings are squashed into a long-term flatness, punctuated by terrible intervals of "dope sickness." With pot, our feelings are altered into a long-term mellowness in which we are convinced of our gentle superiority to others, all the while unaware that nothing important or creative is happening in our lives. We imagine that pot is safe because nothing bad seems to happen on pot. Nothing good happens either—just years and years of…nothing.

ALCOHOL DISTORTS FEELINGS MORE THAN ANY OTHER DRUG

Alcohol gives a wide range of drunken distortions, some of them dose-specific. As our dose of alcohol goes up, our particular distortion of thoughts and feelings may change. I imagine a cartoon of a sign in a bar window: "Happy Hour 5:00–6:00 p.m. Pushy Hour 6:00–7:00 p.m. Argumentative

Hour 7:00–8:00 p.m. Melancholy Hour 8:00–9:00 p.m. Sloppy Hour 9:00–10:00 p.m."

We also slip into drunken ruts that we return to when we drink again. These are not our real selves coming out; these are our drunken selves coming out.

There is the rigid drunk, who is never wrong on any subject, no matter how minor. I knew a man who got angry with his wife for making one too many disappointing dinners. He declared that she would NEVER cook dinner AGAIN! To enforce his imperial will, their new home in the Carolina mountains was built with just a breakfast nook—no kitchen—and they ate out every night. That made it tough when they moved again—potential buyers kept looking for the kitchen—but he was never wrong.

There's the happy drunk, who is the life of the party. There's the romantic drunk, whose bumper sticker reads, "No one is ugly at 2:00 a.m." There's the defiant drunk, whose bumper sticker reads, "Of course I'm drunk. Did you think this is a stunt car?" I saw that man parked on the sidewalk at the Lebanon, New Hampshire, airport. A policeman saw him too, and when he pulled away, the policeman stopped him and arrested him for drunk driving. His lawyer argued that the policeman lacked probable cause for the traffic stop because parking on the sidewalk is not a moving violation. The policeman argued, successfully, that the bumper sticker constituted a public notice: "Of course I'm drunk…"

There's the resentful drunk, whose bumper sticker reads, "Life's a bitch and then you marry one." There's the pitiful drunk. I haven't seen a pitiful bumper sticker, but I've been to pitiful bars, such as the former Blue Star Bar in Saugus, Massachusetts, a dim, diner-shaped building with blue neon lighting and pitiful music on the jukebox: Roy Orbison's "Only the Lonely" and "Crying Over You," Linda Ronstadt's

"Poor Poor Pitiful Me" and "Blue Bayou," and David Frizzel's "I'm Going to Hire a Wino to Decorate Our Home so You'll Stay Home With Me." It's great stuff, and we can sit there and drink and listen to the sad music and drink some more, but at last we've found a place that sounds like we feel—pitiful.

To experience reality, we need brains that are drug and alcohol-free. Any mood-altering chemicals in our brains will perpetuate illusions.

We have magnificent brains, but when they are drugged, unacceptable things become acceptable. Sometimes it is useful to be drugged to accept unacceptable things. For example, during surgery with local anesthetic, with the right combination of drugs, we will lie still and smile while strangers wearing masks cut us with knives. This is something we would not normally accept, but we do so in that situation for our own good.

When recreational drugs are self-administered, the same thing happens: unacceptable things become acceptable. For example, take a man and woman together in a dingy little room with a pile of cocaine, there for an evening of paranoia and impotence, and they'll call it a party. There's no party here. There's no band. The activities are truly dangerous: potential overdose, heart attack, sexually transmitted disease, and the start of some really awful relationships. But if we ask them what they are doing, they'll say, "We're partying."

We have magnificent brains, and when we come to appreciate them, life becomes much more interesting. Many years ago I taught a graduate course in addiction studies at Glassboro State College (now Rowan University) in New Jersey. My favorite guest lecturer was Herr Doctor Professor Wolfgang Vogel, professor of psychoneuropharmacology at Jefferson University Medical School in Philadelphia. He would say to the class:

Class, there is no such thing as the mind. There is only the brain. It is one honey of a computer. It contains millions of separate circuits, tens of thousands of which can run at the same time without becoming unduly confused. It can run for hours on the energy of a single peanut. It is completely mobile [at this point, he would walk the breadth of the classroom] with no external power cord. It can run for sixty to one hundred years with no scheduled maintenance or downtime required. It comes in its own waterproof, shock-resistant container. [Here, he would strike his skull with his fist.] And, best of all, it can be mass-produced inexpensively by unskilled labor!

It is such a wonder that we've all got one! With it, we can think, feel, plan, and take action. When the chemicals are gone, we have a rush of feelings. Unfortunately, many of those feelings hurt. One of my little jokes is that the word "sober" is an acronym. The letters s-o-b-e-r stand for "Son Of a Bitch! Everything's Real!" The first wave of reality is often painful, but if we commit to reality, the second wave isn't so bad, and we can move on to better things. Reality can become our friend.

There are many definitions of mental illness. There are fewer definitions of mental health. My favorite is from George Vaillant: "an unflinching dedication to reality."

GRATITUDE AS A SOURCE OF HOPE

Gratitude gives me a sense of hope.

Vincent van Gogh, who was not actually a good model of recovery, did manage to say, "The best way to know God is to love many things." The more we can let go and allow ourselves to love life and everything in it, the stronger our recovery becomes. George Weller, who was a unit supervisor at Hazelden for many years, said, "Anything worth doing is worth doing poorly." The usual quote ends with "…is worth doing well!" George had a point. If golf is worth playing, before we can play golf well, we have to play golf poorly. We might as well let go of our embarrassment and be grateful for the chance to enjoy playing golf poorly so that we can someday enjoy playing it well.

Life becomes fun when we stop trying to control the outcome of each event. I claim that my life is unmanageable only when I'm trying to manage it. My life isn't meant to be managed, it is meant to be lived. If I work hard at managing my life, something is always slipping out from under my control. If I relax and let God be in charge of my life, I can shift my focus from managing my life to living it. If I live it, I can accept what comes—both advances and setbacks—and get the enjoyment that is available from the good things in life. In recovery, we can get the gift of mindfulness, of living in the day.

A common error that normal people make, as well as alcoholics, is living with 40 percent of our energy in the past in the form of resentment or regret, 40 percent of our energy in the future in the form of anxiety or worry, and only 20 percent of our energy available for the present. As we let go of control and of regret for the past and fear about the future, we live in today. We can spend 5 percent of our energy in the past in the form of respect for our heritage and our story, 5 percent in the future in the form of planning, and 90 percent of our energy for living today. We get to be fully alive right now. Life becomes fun when we trust God and trust the process of recovery. As we let go of our own struggle to control outcomes, we begin to see the humor and the absurdity of life.

Garrison Keillor, who does the radio show *A Prairie Home Companion*, said, "God writes great comedy, but is stuck with poor players who don't know that their lines are funny." When we lack gratitude for sobriety, we cannot notice that our own lines are funny. We can't see the humor in life until we become grateful.

One winter years ago, in the era of videotape rentals, I was at a meeting in the Uptown Club in Saint Paul. It's a large, Victorian-era house with multiple small rooms for small meetings. As the different groups ended, people mingled in the front lobby to meet their friends and go off for coffee or dinner. There was an unhappy woman who was about six months sober and not yet enjoying recovery. She was complaining out loud to no one in particular about having to return three overdue videotapes to Blockbuster Video. She said to the room at large:

"If they think they're going to get four-fifty out of me, they got another think coming. Four-fifty is too much to pay to be overdue just a few hours. Eight o'clock is too early to have to have those tapes back. I had a meeting to go to [as if Blockbuster should care that she had a meeting to go to]. If they think they're going to get four-fifty out of me, I'll show them. I'm going to walk in there and put the tapes on the counter and walk right out, and if anyone says something, I'm never going back there as long as I live."

As she was talking and waving her arms, she backed up and bumped hard into a young man who had a broken neck. He had one of those metal "halo" frames around his head, with the metal bolts screwed into his skull, and a heavy plastic frame on his shoulders. She turned around and looked at him and exclaimed, "What is THAT?"

He said, "I've got a broken neck." At that point, one of his friends came up and said, "How are you, Hal, and how're the bolts in your head?" He laughed and said, "Fine. At least when I've got a screw loose, someone can tighten it!" The group all laughed—except her. Her conversation went like this:

Woman: *"That's terrible! Were you driving drunk?"*

Man: *"No. I was sober four days, ain't that a bitch! I feel lucky."*

Woman: *"Lucky? What's there to feel lucky about?"*

Man: *"One guy got killed. Another's in intensive care. I'm up walking around. Doctor says this will come off in six or eight weeks. I'll end up with just a stiff neck. I feel lucky."*

Woman: *"Lucky? How do you sleep in that?"*

Man: *"In shifts, a little bit at a time."*

(At this, his friends brought his parka. They had split the seams open and sewn Velcro to it so they could paste it together around him. The woman was gradually adjusting to the gruesome reality of a metal halo with bolts drilled into his skull. Finally she spoke.)

Woman: *"Well, I guess you have a point. It might have been worse."*

Friend of the man: "Yeah, they could have charged you six dollars!" (At that point, everybody but the woman was laughing.)

When we learn to receive our lives with gratitude, our stories actually are funny. If an outsider stood outside any Twelve Step meeting, they would be amazed at our laughter. I am grateful to be alive, to be free of the tyranny of active addiction, and so much more. I am grateful for Priscilla, with whom I am happy to get old. I am grateful for sober friends, with whom I can share a sense of adventure and a sense of the absurd. I am grateful for my children and grandchildren, who demonstrate that the story of my childhood does not have to be repeated through the generations. I am grateful for my Twelve Step programs, where I have been received without questions and supported without limits. I am grateful for the Hazelden Family Program, where I began my adventure of recovery in 1987, and grateful for God, who never leaves us alone and without a friend in the world.

TRANSFORMATION AS A SOURCE OF HOPE

Transformation is different from change. Change is something we can do. We can change our socks. We can change a tire. With some effort, we can even change our minds. With practice, we can change our behavior. Transformation is bigger than change. Transformation is something that God does for us that we cannot do for ourselves. In transformation we find hope.

With alcoholism and addiction we need more than change, we need transformation. I tried to change. I tried to change my drinking problem and my drug problem by quitting. I quit. I quit again. My estimate is that I quit twenty-three times. The trouble is, I started using again twenty-four times. So much for change. Then I tried to change by cutting down my intake. I did change by cutting down my intake. That allowed me to settle for less out of life, so I did. I settled for a lot less. Many of us can change our patterns of alcohol and drug use enough to keep it going for many years. That is not transformation.

Transformation happens when God takes something that is truly bad, turns it inside out, and transforms it into something that is all good. Transformation is radical and complete. To get an idea of how radical and how complete transformation can be, I suggest a look at the Christian symbol and the actual reality of a cross. What's a cross in its original setting? It's a tool for executing people very slowly, so they suffer a whole lot before they die. It is a tool for inflicting vengeance, hatred, and punishment on people before killing them. It is also a useful tool for terrifying the people who watch the process into strict obedience to the dictator who ordered the cross put in place. So, as a reality and as a symbol, it's all bad. There is no good side or redeeming feature to a cross. However, God has taken this evil thing and transformed it until it is now suitable for jewelry for little girls. What has happened here?

To get an idea of how extreme this transformation is, imagine a religion whose central symbol was an electric chair. On Sundays, there would be a table in the front of the church with a white cloth and a gold-plated electric chair. On communion Sundays, we could place a Barbie doll in the electric chair and zap her. Then the congregation could stand and sing a favorite hymn:

So I'll cherish my old electric chair,
'til my trophies at last I lay down.
And I'll cling to that old 'lectric chair,
'til I exchange it some day for a crown.

We'd say they were sick. But that's essentially what's happened here. God has transformed this tool of hatred and death into a symbol of kindness and mercy. The Red Cross today carries out acts of rescue and mercy. The Blue Cross provides health insurance. Industrial safety is promoted by the Green Cross Association. Health and welfare ministries of the churches are conducted under the banner of the Gold Cross Association. Something that was all bad has become good.

WHAT DOES TRANSFORMATION HAVE TO DO WITH US?

The Twelve Steps include a plan in which God transforms the bad things about us into a source of power for recovery. In Step Five we admit to God, to ourselves, and to another human being the exact nature of our wrongs. We write out in Step Four and we speak out in Step Five exactly what is bad about us. This is where the Twelve Step programs are different from church. The church's answer at this point is that we should be forgiven. The Twelve Step answer is that we should be transformed. Here's how:

In Step Five we have told God the plain truth about our wrongs. In Step Six we become entirely ready for God to transform us. We don't change ourselves; we are transformed by God. Here's exactly how that works:

Cling to the thought that, in God's hands, the dark past
is the greatest possession you have—the key to life and

happiness for others. With it you can avert death and misery for them. (Alcoholics Anonymous, p. 124)

Instead of seeking to have our wrongs washed away, or trying to put them behind us, we offer our wrongs to God, to let God use our wrongs and use us to save other alcoholics and addicts from misery and death. In A.A's suggested Seventh Step prayer, we offer God all of us, good and bad, and we pray that God will remove from us every defect of character that stands in the way of our usefulness to God and our fellows. But it is the defects of character that are removed, not the wrongs.

A time will come when we will meet a suffering alcoholic or addict who is just like us. Because the thing that has been bad about us is the same thing that is bad about them, we will be uniquely qualified to help them. Our dark past is the same as their dark past, and we will hold the key to their life and happiness. We will be able to avert death and misery for them by sharing the truth about ourselves, sharing our stories. That is what God will be calling us to do. In the very moment that we help them, what has always been bad about us will be transformed into an expression of God's power and love, and we will be transformed along with it. I have experienced this, and helping others has given me great hope.

ANGELS AS A SOURCE OF HOPE

Angels give me a sense of hope. I think of two kinds of angels. The first is the kind most of us have in mind. I have a lovely angel print in my office. If you look on the Web, it's "Angel" by Abbott Handerson Thayer, an American artist who lived from 1849 to 1921. I'm fond of Thayer's angel, and I even visit her on the second floor of the National Museum of American Art when I am in Washington, DC. She is as angels are usually portrayed: an otherworldly being with a white toga and white wings.

There is another meaning for the word *angel* that is every bit as human as you or I. The ancient Greek word *Angelos* and the ancient Hebrew word *Malach* both mean "angel," but they also both mean "messenger." In that sense, "angel" is a job description, like "librarian" or "fire fighter." A librarian is someone who catalogs and maintains a library. A fire fighter is someone who fights fires. Any person who carries a message of hope to us from our Higher Power is functioning as our angel. They may not be personally angelic, or even spiritual. They are carrying out a job on behalf of God. They may not even know they are doing God's work. They are just doing it.

Once we come to believe there is a Power greater than ourselves who can and will restore us to sanity, then it is reasonable that this Higher Power would try to do it. It is rare for God to show up in a white-light experience. More often, God sends human angels with messages of hope. The disease of addiction tries to set up an effective barrier in the brain against hearing any hope, but God keeps on sending messengers and messages. Often, only when we look back over our lives do we recognize them.

In the 1980s I was a copastor with Priscilla of four small churches in rural New England. I would go to the local post office to get our mail from a little bronze post office box with a dial lock on it. The post office was a gathering point for the town. While there, I would sometimes run into a woman named Sheila, who attended one of the churches. She was chemically dependent, anorexic, promiscuous, and anxious.

Whenever she saw me, she would pour out all her troubles, there in the post office, oblivious to the fact that she was entertaining the postal workers, who worked behind these post office boxes, with her ongoing soap opera.

One day as she was pouring out a number of troubles, I asked her to pick just one problem she was having trouble with, then go and ask God for help with just that one thing, and then see what happened. She said, "I need help slowing down. I gotta go!" And she left.

Three days later I saw her there again. I asked: "Did you ask—" "Yes!" "Did anything—" "I got a speeding ticket for fifty-three in a thirty zone!" "Where did you—" "Up by Ron's Garage!"

I said, "Sheila, you've lived in this town for fifteen years. You've had ample opportunity to learn that the one cop who works days sits in the bushes up by Ron's Garage. So he sees you coming, you look like a hot prospect, and he flips on the radar. It reads 'five-three.' Then what happens? A uniformed messenger hands you a note that says, 'Slow down.' What did you want from your Higher Power?"

Another time, it was Sunday afternoon. I had preached in two churches, as had Priscilla. She was making Sunday dinner, and I was reading the *New York Times*. It was peaceful. I suddenly sat up bolt upright, agitated, and said to Priscilla, "I have to go to [the other town, eight miles away]." She asked why, and I said I didn't know, but I HAD to go. I drove the eight miles, fearing the worst. I was on the local rescue squad, and I was sensing some kind of disaster. Some years before, a plane had crashed on a neighboring mountain, and I envisioned that, or a fire—certainly grave danger.

I got to the other town and there was…nothing. Nothing at all. There stood the church, the senior center, and the village green with the bandstand, all in place. I was sitting in my car wondering if I was even crazier than normal when a woman who belonged to that church drove down the hill, through two stop signs, and out onto the state highway. I followed her. She sped up. I sped up. Finally she stopped when she reached the S curves east of town. I stopped behind her, walked up like a traffic cop, and tapped on her window. She rolled it down an inch.

I asked, "Why am I following you?" She said, "I was going to kill myself. I left a note for the children." I said, "Would you come for coffee with me instead?" She said "No." I thought, *What do I do now?* I said, "Well, I'm not going away!"

Finally she agreed to go to coffee with me. We sat and talked a long time. It turned out that the common theme in all her problems was alcohol. She ended up joining A.A. It's been over twenty years, and she's sober and happy. Am I particularly angelic? Don't count on it. It wasn't my talent that made God call on me, it was my availability. I could be agitated to get up and go, and I did.

There's one more important example. When I was about six years old, I got abused once again. My abuser knelt on my chest, punched my eyes in, and broke both cheekbones and my nose at the same time. Both eyeballs were squashed into their sockets, and I passed out.

I woke up in the emergency room. The ER was worse than the original beating. Everybody grabbed a piece of me. I was crazed and fighting them, and they were crazy and fighting me and trying to stick tubes in my face, trying to hold me down, and I passed out again. When I came to, I freaked out because it was pitch dark and terribly cold. I thought they had misdiagnosed me as dead and put me in the cooler, so

I screamed and fought against the cot restraints. They came and got me. They pushed the cot into a little dark room.

A woman was there, probably a nurse, whose job it was to put cold compresses on my eyes to shrink the swelling. My wrists were tied to the cot. She would run a terry-cloth washcloth under the cold water tap, partially wring it out, and place it gently on my eyes to reduce the swelling. When it got warm, she would put it back in the cold water flow and then repeat the process.

She told me that if I promised not to touch my face, she would untie my hands. I was too swollen to talk, but I said "uh-huh," and she untied my hands. After she had reduced the swelling, she sat with me and held my hand and comforted me. She touched my arm with her other hand. This was very strange, and wonderful, for I had no memory of being touched in a kindly way. She sat with me a long time, comforting me. I fell asleep and woke up, and she was still there. I fell asleep again and woke again, and she was still there, comforting me with both of her hands on my arms. Never before had someone sat with me when I was hurt; I was always left to hurt alone. I couldn't see her, but I absorbed her kindness as deeply as I could, because I wanted it so much. Later I woke up when a group of men came in and said, "Well, what do we have here?" What they had was a real mess, and I went off to surgery. I never encountered her again.

That began a long, excruciatingly boring summer, probably six to eight weeks long. I was in the hospital, in a six-bed pediatrics room, in the mid-1950s. My eyes were bandaged, so I couldn't see anything. There was no television or radio, no air conditioning—just fans—and there was nothing whatever to do. I had no visitors the whole time. Each afternoon, sick boys would come in to have their tonsils taken out. Their parents would fuss over them; they would be cranky and afraid, and the next morning they would go to surgery and not return. I would hear footsteps and not know who was coming or what they would do. Sometimes they would feed me or give me a bedpan or give me a shot or bathe me. Usually they did not introduce themselves or tell me what they were going to do. They mostly didn't talk to me; they just did things to me. Some nurses were kind, some were unkind, and some were just brisk and efficient, but when I heard footsteps, I didn't know who or what was coming, and I was scared, with no one to comfort me. The endless boredom was the hardest part, especially because I didn't know how long I had been there or how long I would be there. I didn't know if anyone would ever come for me. For my self-defense, I later forgot the whole thing.

Almost thirty-five years later, I was at the psychiatrist's office, trying to recover from post-traumatic stress disorder. He listened to other stories, because I didn't remember that one. He said, "Now we have enough abuse stories to know why you turned into a dangerous sociopath—except you didn't. So where did the kindness come into your life? You cannot have something you never learned. You cannot speak German if you have never heard German spoken. So where did you learn kindness?"

I said I didn't know, because I sure didn't learn it at home. He said it was important that I remember because I needed to own that side of myself. I still couldn't remember. Then I remembered her.

This unknown nurse is a huge part of my life today. She touched my soul that night, as well as my arm, and changed me. She was a messenger from God, bearing a message that kindness and care exist in this world. Many years later, when

I read in the A.A.'s Big Book an invitation in Step Three to turn my will and my life over to the care of God, I had already learned about that care from her. She was my angel.

TWO QUESTIONS ABOUT ANGELS

The first of two important questions about angels is this: Who has already been your angel or angels? Who has already carried a message of hope to you from God? Who has shown you love? Who has told you that your life matters? Who has shown you that recovery is possible for you? Your angels have already been there, and it is important for you to find them and take them into your heart. Let us look back and find our angels.

The second question is this: to whom are we being called to become their angels? Our Twelve Step programs call on us to become angels. Step Twelve of A.A. says:

Having had a spiritual awakening as the result of these steps, we tried to carry this message to alcoholics, and to practice these principles in all our affairs. (Alcoholics Anonymous, p. 60)

That's us: message carriers who have had a spiritual awakening as the result of the steps we have taken. As we carry a message of hope to the alcoholics or addicts who still suffer, we are functioning as their angels. Hope flows through us as we pass it on to them.

If we practice acceptance of reality, practice finding our gratitude, are alert for transformation in ourselves and others, and are willing to both receive angels and become angels, our hope will endure for a lifetime.

CHAPTER 8:

FINDING JOY IN LIFE

Since 1976, I have been helping alcoholics and addicts find solutions to their problems. During that time, I have also been trying to solve my own problems. Those parallel tracks have involved focusing mostly on problems and solutions to those problems.

Even in recovery, we tend to focus on unresolved issues, with the expectation that if we could resolve all our unresolved issues, we would be fine. It's as if we start off with a very low negative number as our score in life and then relentlessly work our way up to zero.

If we envision recovery simply as working our way out of our problems, we probably will become discouraged and will be at risk of giving up. The truth is that two different things are going on at the same time: our troubles are becoming less, and we are also beginning to find joy in life, even while our troubles are still substantial.

GOD WANTS US TO BE FREE, JOYOUS, HAPPY

There is a whole realm of positive spirituality available to us that is much more than the relief of distress. The Twelve Step programs do not focus merely on getting drug-free. They offer a way of life that is tremendously more satisfying than using chemicals—and also a whole lot more satisfying than the so-called "normal" way of life.

In *Narcotics Anonymous*, NA's basic text, it says:

> *If we had written down our list of expectations when we came to the program, we would have been cheating ourselves. Hopeless living problems have become joyously changed. Our disease has been arrested, and now anything is possible. We become increasingly open-minded and open to new ideas in all areas of our lives. (p.106)*

One sentence from A.A.'s Big Book keeps repeating in my mind since the first time I read it: "We are sure God wants us to be happy, joyous, and free." (p.133) First, *they* were sure. Now *I* am sure.

In recovery, we are not content with a ceremonial God who shows up at funerals, listens to us swear on a Bible in court, and is called on to comfort us in the face of disaster. Instead, we have a God who offers us a path from despair to hope, from dishonesty to honesty, from fear to trust, from addiction to recovery, and from misery to happiness.

We have a God who breaks into life when no one expects it, bringing an escape from an unsolvable problem, a sudden insight, a new way of life, and often a good joke. We are sure God wants us to be happy, joyous, and free.

As I wrote in the first chapter, "Staying Sober," I do not mean to blow off serious questions about good and evil. There are still three sources of bad things in life: randomness, error, and evil. We continue to encounter these, even in recovery, and yet I agree with the Big Book where it says we are sure that God wants us to be happy, joyous, and free. It doesn't say we will always be happy, joyous, and free, but it does say God wants us to be that way. I want to be that way, too, so we are in agreement, and I'm willing to work together with God to have that come true and to help others have it come true in their lives, as well.

I still have reasons to be miserable. I have experiences of torture stuck in my mind that are hard to forget and hard to mitigate. Normal people can't bear to hear about them, so I don't ask them to listen. There are several centers for survivors of torture in North America, but none of them treat people who are citizens of the United States or Canada. We have conveniently defined torture as something that only happens to third-world peoples who live under dictators. My range of sleep experiences varies from no dreams, through bad dreams, to vivid nightmares. I hear songs about "sweet dreams," but I have never had one. I have more complaints, but even I don't want to hear my own complaints.

If I dwell on reasons to be miserable, my misery comes into sharp relief and becomes the most prominent feature of my days and nights. In the midst of these problems, here comes A.A.'s Big Book talking about merriment:

> *"So we think cheerfulness and laughter make for usefulness. Outsiders are sometimes shocked when we bust into merriment over a seemingly tragic experience out of the past. But why shouldn't we laugh? We have recovered, and have been given the power to help others…We are sure God wants us to be happy, joyous, and free." (pp. 132–3)*

Once a month I give my recovery story in thirty minutes during the 7:00 p.m. patient lecture at Hazelden. I have only thirty minutes to tell the story, so I tell how I got addicted to alcohol and drugs in order to treat the pain of abuse. I tell how I got so addicted that I became immobilized. I tell how I left college broke, unemployed, and homeless. I tell my recovery story too—also in those same thirty minutes. I tell it with a lot of humor. People find themselves laughing one minute, then saying to themselves, "I shouldn't be laughing, that's terrible" the next, then laughing again. Sometimes they ask me if it is OK that they laughed, and I read them this passage from the Big Book: "Why shouldn't we laugh? We have recovered, and have been given the power to help others."

WE HAVE RECOVERED

We have recovered and have been given the power to help others. We have recovered if we did not drink or drug today. I do not keep score in terms of months or years in recovery. Today I have a twenty-four-year medallion. I carry it everywhere. I put my hand in my pocket to literally "be in touch with my recovery," but it does not make me more sober than a twenty-four-hour medallion would. If we did not drink or drug today, we have recovery, and we have some experience, strength, and hope to share with others.

How do we know we have recovered? Before recovery, we could not go a day without alcohol or drugs. Now we can. We have a program, a Higher Power, a peer group, Twelve Steps, and each other to surround us on our way.

THE POWER TO HELP OTHERS

The power to help others lies at the intersection of our stories and our understanding of God at work in our lives. Many of us know our stories, once we are awake enough to remember them. When we realize how God has been doing for us what we could not do for ourselves, we will find joy, happiness, and a fairy tale worth telling.

Years ago I read a book on preaching titled *Telling the Truth: The Gospel as Tragedy, Comedy, and Fairy Tale,* by Frederick Buechner. He wrote that to preach the Christian Gospel, it had to be understood as a drama with a sad ending (tragedy); a drama with a happy ending (comedy); and a drama with a wildly improbable, comic, wonderfully happy ending (fairy tale). In a fairy tale, he wrote, the frog *does* turn into a prince, the straw *does* turn into gold, and other miracles happen at just the right moment. Once we realize that our stories of addiction and recovery have these elements—tragedy, comedy, and fairy tale—then our stories will have the power to help others.

THE POWER OF STORIES

Isaac Bashevis Singer, who won the Nobel Prize in Literature in 1978, once wrote, "God loves stories, so he created people!" A.A. says our stories disclose what we were like, what happened, and what we are like now. Many of our stories are so amazing that they *are* fairy tales come true.

THE OUT-OF-CONTROL LAWYER

In the Silkworth unit's Step Two and Three group, I sometimes ask if anyone has a story about how he got into treatment.

This story, offered by a lawyer, stretches the boundaries of luck to the breaking point.

He had been using methamphetamine, and his life had gone way downhill. Another meth user, whom he barely knew, was living in his condo because his wife had moved out. One evening when they were both running out of meth, the other man's meth dealer came to collect a bad debt from the roommate. The roommate couldn't pay, and the dealer began to beat the roommate with a hammer. The lawyer was frightened, not of the violence, but of the disgrace that would come to him if a roommate was found murdered in his home. He was thinking, *I can't have a murder in my apartment. I've got to get them out of here.* He solved the problem by getting them into his car and driving them away.

Now he was thinking, *I can't have a murder in my car, either, because there will be blood all over!* He was driving along the Black Horse Pike in Southern New Jersey at 3:00 a.m. It's a divided highway with traffic lights and strip malls. He pulled into an empty parking lot and turned the car off. He opened the back seat and tried to haul the dealer with the hammer off of the victim. At that point, another car's headlights came on. It was a police car, and the officer shouted, "Freeze." The lawyer broke away and ran straight for the police car, opened the back seat, and jumped in. He said he was never so happy to see a cop in his life.

I asked him, "Have you ever heard that phrase, 'There's never a cop around when you need one'?" He said, "That's not the weird part!" I asked what the weird part was. He said, "It was the chief of police!" It turned out that the police chief hadn't been able to sleep. He was tossing and turning. He finally got up, put on his dress uniform, and went down to the police station. He found nothing going on there, so he signed out a police car and drove around. He found nothing, so he pulled into a vacant lot and turned off the lights, wondering, *What am I doing up at three a.m.?* One minute later, the lawyer pulled in with the drug dealer beating the roommate with a hammer, so the chief arrested them.

The lawyer got out on bail and came straight to treatment. He said, "I think God is trying to tell me to get straight."

AN ENCOUNTER IN PHANG NGA BAY

Priscilla and I are fond of the Aman Resorts. Our favorite is Amanpuri, in Phuket, Thailand. One time we were on a small excursion boat with about eighteen people in Phang Nga Bay. It is a lovely area, with large rock formations. It was a scene in one of the James Bond movies. I was wearing swim trunks and a T shirt from "Hanley-Hazelden," a treatment center in West Palm Beach, Florida, that was jointly operated at the time by Hazelden and the Hanley Foundation.

One of the men who was an Amanpuri guest came up to me, quite drunk, and said, "I need to go to Hanley-Hazelden." We had a good talk about his drinking problem. I wondered if he was in a blackout and would remember nothing, but there's no way to know, so we talked, alcoholic to alcoholic. It turned out he lived in Palm Beach, a few miles from the center. He was a bit confused, but he said at one point, "Let's do it!" So, I pointed him to the satellite phone, and he called in a reservation. I gave him my business card and asked him to send me a postcard when he got there.

I didn't really expect to hear from him. A few weeks later, I got a nice letter from him. He wrote that he came out of a blackout with my card in his pocket. Then he got an e-mail from his secretary telling him he had a reservation at Hanley-Hazelden. He decided to keep the reservation and go there. He thanked me for "saving his life." I wrote back that I was just a small part of God's plan for him, and I wished him well.

HOW TO FIND JOY IN LIFE

We take the Twelve Steps, initially, to get sober. We continue with those steps to become spiritually fit. When we truly surrender ourselves to God and continue the steps in that spirit, we find joy along the way.

First we discover that spiritual principles will solve all our problems. Then we allow God's spirit to flow into us. How this happens is that we keep our minds open to the insights God has for us. All day long, in small matters and large ones, we ask ourselves this question, "What does God want me to do about this?"

Eventually, we don't even ask the question in words. It becomes a state of mind, a sense of anticipation. We know there will be wonderful opportunities ahead for us to be in tune with God. I had a foretaste of this when I was a student at Hazelden in 1989.

In the Clinical Pastoral Education program that existed at that time, we were supposed to write a Theology of Ministry paper. It was widely understood that this paper would be around seventy-five to a hundred pages long and would draw on the work of major theologians and the traditions of Clinical Pastoral Education. The other students worked long and hard on their papers. I have never been a very good student. Scholarship and I don't get along.

I was sitting at the computer, looking at a blank screen. I thought, *Theology comes from "theos," "logos," or "talking about God." So what do I have to say about our relationship with God?* For my Theology of Ministry paper, I wrote four sentences on one sheet of paper. They were:

1. Show up.
2. Pay attention.
3. God will do something good.
4. Try to be part of it, or at least admire it when it happens.

I turned it in. The paper was accepted, much to the dismay of my fellow students. I still use that as my plan for the day.

I do make plans. I have a calendar with plans on it that go well into next year. What I don't plan are outcomes. I do my part in life and try to trust God for the outcome.

Finding joy in life comes from showing up for life; being aware of God's presence in our lives; trusting God to do good things; and trying to cooperate with God in bringing joy, happiness, recovery, freedom from addiction, justice, mercy, healing, love, and every good thing to life.

Today, I take the first three steps every morning before I get involved with other people. I say to myself, "Good morning, John. You're an alcoholic. Pay attention!" That is Step Oone. I then remember there is a God and it isn't me. That is Step Two. I ask that God direct my motives and guide my day. That is Step Three. This takes just a few minutes, but it makes all the difference in my life. Without it, I am likely to revert to "natural." "Natural" is the natural self-centeredness of the alcoholic. The fundamental choice in my life every day is between self-centeredness and the experience of being guided all through the day by an awareness of God in my life.

By holding on to this awareness, each encounter with another human being holds unknown possibilities. Many encounters hold only the possibility of a brief kindness. However, even that is so much more valuable than the brief hostility or brief indifference I used to offer to the world. I don't know which encounters will have within them the opportunity to be of genuine service or to show real love, so I try to hold myself in a state of readiness, to be used by God for good. Then, when I get a chance to make a difference, the result is joy and happiness.

We carry a message of hope to the alcoholic and addict who still suffers. Sometimes the message results in change, sometimes the message falls flat. I've heard at meetings, "Carry the message, not the alcoholic." We are responsible for trying to be of service—not for the alcoholic or addict's response to that message. God has lots of other people to use if we fail.

"IN-FLIGHT ENTERTAINMENT"

I had a spiritual-care consult with an angry Silkworth patient. He had a common but difficult combination of being angry with God and not believing in God. It's useless to bring up the inherent contradiction of being angry at someone who doesn't exist, so I listened. He was angry at God because he was a "born-again Christian" who had lived through a near-death experience. We believed he had tried to commit suicide, although he denied it.

He had swallowed a whole bottle of pain-killers and then called his brother to say good-bye. The brother called the police, who broke into his apartment and sent him to the hospital. It was a close call. His heart stopped in the ambulance and was restarted in the emergency room. He went into a coma for a couple of days. He had transferred directly to Hazelden from the hospital. Now he was angry at God because he had had a near-death experience but had not had any visions of God, angels, or heaven.

He had heard testimonies in church of other people with near-death experiences who had seen white light, a tunnel of light, or an angel coming to welcome them, and he had seen nothing but blackness. Now he demanded an explanation for this deficit from me, whom he regarded as God's spokesman.

I said I didn't know, because God doesn't tell me everything, but it seemed to me that perhaps the reason he didn't get a vision of light was that dying wasn't God's plan for him that day—it was his plan. Perhaps the lack of a vision was God's way of saying that the door to heaven was closed to him at that time. He was meant to live and recover. At the right time, he might see an angel or light or whatever God had planned for him, but this wasn't the right time. That seemed plausible to me, but it didn't satisfy him at all.

The next morning was Step Two and Three Group on Silkworth, and he slammed his protest down in front of the group. He demanded I give him an answer to this terrible spiritual problem that was keeping him from recovering.

I said: "I agree that this is a spiritual problem. The name of this spiritual problem is ingratitude. You don't have any gratitude that your brother called the police. You don't have any gratitude that the police kicked in your door and rescued you. You don't have any gratitude that the rescue squad kept you breathing and your heart beating on the way to the hospital. You don't have any gratitude that the emergency room jump-started your heart. You don't have any gratitude that you made the perilous flight three days through the coma in the intensive care unit. You're sitting here complaining about the quality of the in-flight entertainment. Be glad you survived the flight. You don't get to pick the movie!"

The peer group laughed at him. He did not seem to benefit from this insight. He stayed mad at God, me, and the peer group. He left treatment at twenty-eight days without appearing to have benefited from it. All I could say is that God wasn't finished with him yet. I simply prayed that he would hear the message of recovery some other way.

ANOTHER IN-FLIGHT INSPIRATION

Back in 2002 I was flying from Minneapolis to Boston on Northwest Airlines. I was in seat 2B in First Class, across from the galley bulkhead. They were doing the "full flight–one carry-on bag" announcement. At the last minute, a drunken man came on board, dragging two overstuffed carry-on bags. The flight attendant, who in this case happened to be a man, stepped in front of him and said, "Sir, you can only bring one carry-on aboard because the bins are full. Frankly, I don't think you will find room for even one, but you can look."

The drunk snarled, "I'm not checking my f----'n bag, I paid for my ticket, and I get two bags, and that's it!" The flight attendant stepped in front of him in the aisle and said, "Sir! I have to check one of those bags." With that, the drunk grabbed the flight attendant by his jacket and slammed him into the bulkhead right across from me. I thought, *This isn't going to go well.*

Hearing the noise, the pilot came out and said, "We're not taking you anywhere. Now get off this plane." The drunk said, "I'm not getting off this f---ing plane. I paid for my ticket and…" The argument continued. The copilot probably called for help because in about two minutes, a police truck pulled up and two policemen and a dog came up the Jetway to the door of the plane.

Policeman: "Sir. Step off of the plane and talk to me."

Drunk: "I'm not getting off of this f---ing plane. If you want me, you come get me."

Policeman: "If I have to come get you, I'm going to mace you and set the dog on you. Now you get off that plane."

Drunk: "No!"

With that, the police stepped on the plane, sprayed the man in the face with a mace pen, and let the dog loose. The dog jumped on him and bit him in the shoulder. I was wondering, *How does the dog know who to bite?* They were all wrestling right next to me, and the drunk was kicking me as they cuffed him and wrenched him to his feet.

The punch line was just sitting there, so I took out a Hazelden business card and offered it, saying, "If something about this evening's drinking proves unsatisfying, please feel free to call us." He couldn't take it because he was cuffed, but one policeman said, "I'll give it to him," and they laughed.

I thought that was it. Eight years later, I was giving a talk in another city and told the story, mostly as a joke. One of my listeners said, "I know that guy!" I asked if the man had ever come to Hazelden. My listener said no, the man had gone on drinking for several years, but he had gone to treatment in that city and was now in A.A. He had told that airline story as an example of how God was trying to tell him to get help, but he wasn't ready to listen. He got help through someone else years later. But I did help plant a seed of doubt about his drinking, and later he did reach out for help.

(Incidentally, I found out how the dog knows whom to bite: the dog bites the person who smells like mace.)

OPENING TO JOY AND HAPPINESS

Part of finding joy in life is opening to it. This comes with recovery. I inadvertently did a research project on this. When I was still drinking, Priscilla and I went to Amanpuri in Thailand, our favorite resort. I was able to identify that it was a wonderful place, but I experienced it as if I were an emotionally detached travel writer. I carefully catalogued the many ways it exceeded the standards of any beach resort we had ever seen. I could have told you dozens of details about it, until you were bored from listening, but I didn't actually enjoy being there. I drank too many excellent drinks from their magnificent bar. I sat at that bar and identified the flowers, the colors of the ocean, the texture of the sand, and the way just a little bit of water was allowed to cool the black marble around the pool, and did not get one bit of actual enjoyment out of the experience. Alcohol, Valium, and Percodan made it impossible to feel anything. The resort was right there, but I was experiencing it through a feelings-proof filter. God was right there too, but the idea of God never occurred to me.

We returned when I was two years sober. Amanpuri hadn't changed, but I had. I could now have feelings, though I didn't trust them. I felt tastes and temperatures, the massages, and some love for Priscilla. I even was aware of God, but all these feelings made me nervous.

We returned again when I was ten years sober, and I went YES! I felt joy and happiness being there with Priscilla. God was there too. Everything had been there all along, but I had not been ready to feel it. The resort was the same. Joy and happiness were waiting for me to find them. Now the lovely view from that bar is my screen saver on my computer and iPhone. It no longer reminds me of getting drunk; it reminds me of serenity and happiness.

SURPRISED BY GOD

Last year, when I had a speaking engagement in New York City, I visited with an old friend who lives there whose father had just died. She, too, is a recovering alcoholic. She, too, sees God in her life on a daily basis, but she was tired. She had grown up unloved by her parents. She held on to hope through her teenage years. She thought there was a family expectation that she would go to college. When she finished high school, her parents told her they weren't going to pay for anything more for her at all. She left home and worked her way into a career. She was always the "less than" daughter. Her mother had died years ago, and her father died two weeks before, after a long, pitiless illness. We spent a Saturday together in Manhattan.

We went walking. We had lunch in Chinatown, in a basement restaurant. We walked along the Bowery and through Greenwich Village. In Washington Square Park, we saw excellent musicians and great acrobats. We took two buses to Central Park and walked past the dairy and the ball fields into the mall. The mall has a canopy of beautiful American elm trees. We walked toward the Bethesda Fountain, which has a large angel sculpture, a remembrance of the angel who stirred the waters at the biblical pool of Bethesda. It was at that first Bethesda fountain that Jesus asked the question that echoes through the centuries, "Do you want to be healed?"

As we got to the covered terrace just before the fountain, we stopped to observe a couple in their fifties getting married in the shaded corner of the terrace. They were clearly in love and were attended by their children on both sides. It was a simple, moving ceremony. Just beyond them, in the shadows of the terrace, an inner-city children's choir was singing spiritual songs. They were boys and girls ages about ten to thirteen. They had a cardboard box out for donations and to sell compact discs. They were an unintended musical setting for the wedding, and their music echoed wonderfully in the underground terraces. It seemed to me that the hand of God was on the park, because it was so peaceful, so serene, so blessed. We came out of the pavilion, toward the fountain, and my friend began to cry, and cry. I put my arm around her without speaking.

"It's just joy," she said after a while. "I'm overwhelmed by joy." And I cried with her.

Sometimes today's story is a tragedy, and all we can do is mourn. Sometimes today's story is a comedy, and we rejoice at the happy ending. Sometimes today's story is a fairy tale, and we are amazed.

AN ALCOHOLICS ANONYMOUS FAIRY TALE

One of my friends works at a famous medical school. She found an original 1939 red A.A. Big Book that the medical school library had thrown out. Bill Wilson sent the first Big Books to medical school libraries in the hope that the medical community would take an interest in this new movement. The medical school library got it in 1939, and in seventy years, no one had checked it out, and so it was discarded. My friend rescued it from the trash pile and gave it to me. The title page reads, "How more than one hundred men have recovered from alcoholism."

The group who published the book had hope that their work would result in more alcoholics finding recovery. When they finished the first 164 pages, which constitute the basic text of Alcoholics Anonymous, they needed a way to close their message. This is what they wrote:

Abandon yourself to God as you understand God. Admit your faults to him and to your fellows. Clear away the wreckage of your past. Give freely of what you find and join us. We shall be with you in the Fellowship of the Spirit, and you will surely meet some of us as you trudge the road of Happy Destiny. May God bless you and keep you—until then. (Alcoholics Anonymous, p. 164)

The fairy tale continues. The group of one hundred men has grown. According to the 2012 General Service Conference of Alcoholics Anonymous, there are now an estimated 1,384,699 members of Alcoholics Anonymous in the United States and Canada. People are finding joy in the rooms of all the Twelve Step programs. If we keep taking the first three steps every day, we will keep finding joy in our lives.

CHAPTER 9:

BECOMING HAPPY

How do we become happy in sobriety? Happiness is not a decision; it is the result of the process of recovery that is outlined here—that is, the process that the Twelve Step programs teach us. Happiness can also be achieved by other programs or religions that lead us away from self-centeredness and toward service to God and other people.

Many authors, speakers, and spiritual leaders tell us that happiness is up to us. If we think happy thoughts, we will become happy. If we visualize happiness, we will attract happiness to us. If we claim prosperity, we will become prosperous. If we meditate on health, we will defeat disease. It all sounds cheerful. The unfortunate byproduct of that philosophy is that if, after thinking happy thoughts, we still have some unhappiness, it is then our own fault for not choosing to be happy.

True happiness is grounded in reality, including an awareness of suffering and of our own flaws. Carl Jung, the psychiatrist, wrote, "One does not become enlightened by imagining figures of light, but by making the darkness conscious." To experience happiness, we also have to be familiar with its absence.

We become happy by staying sober. We become happy by developing our spirituality, by learning to surrender to a Higher Power, and by trusting in that Higher Power. We become happy by practicing the spiritual principles of our program. We become happy by inviting our Higher Power to heal the injuries to our souls. We become happy by learning to love people, instead of just wanting them. We become happy when we embrace hope and find joy in life. The process of becoming happy has quietly been going on in the background of our lives while we have been doing the work of recovery and seeking the guidance of our Higher Power.

THE PROMISES OF RECOVERY

There is a well-loved passage in A.A.'s Big Book (pp. 83–84) that has come to be known as "The Promises of Recovery." They were written, I believe, to give the newcomer to A.A. something to look forward to. As I look at these promises again, they are a record of how I have become happy. Below, I describe how each of them has come true for me. They may trace your path to happiness, as well.

"We are going to know a new freedom
and a new happiness."

One essential element of all addiction is the loss of freedom. When I was drinking and drugging, I imagined I was a free man. I had an exaggerated sense of freedom. I had a small Gadsen Flag on my desk. The Gadsen Flag is still an official flag of the United States, dating from the Revolutionary War. It has a bright yellow field, a green coiled snake, and black letters that spell out: "Don't Tread on Me." That was part of my self-image: a free man, a revolutionary, coiled to strike, dangerous. That powerful self-image was a long way from the pitiful drunk who threw up every morning on the way to the bus stop.

I imagined I was free to drink or not drink. I knew for a fact that I could quit any time I wanted to. I now estimate that I quit twenty-three or twenty-four times, which at the time proved to my complete satisfaction that I could quit! I was, however, powerless to keep from returning to alcohol and drug use. I had lost my freedom, and after a while there was no more point in pretending. Only when I got sober for good could I find this new freedom and a new happiness.

I recently had a breakthrough at Hazelden with George, a sixty-year-old man in treatment, who was committed by a court in his home county down south. This man had been terribly alcoholic for decades, but he had never come to understand the nature of his alcoholism and had relapsed many times. He came to my attention because he was the only patient in many years whose insurance company called the treatment provider he'd been using to say that he needed a *higher* level of care, not less care. It was the insurance company that insisted he be transferred to Hazelden. This alone was remarkable.

George was a respected married professional man who had lived in the same town all his life. Politically, he was a conservative Republican with traditional values. I explained to him that, under the Constitution, a court cannot deprive him of his liberty unless he is convicted of a crime, and he, George, had not committed any crime. There is one exception to this constitutional rule. The judge in his hometown could deprive George of his liberty if someone has shown the judge, by clear and convincing medical evidence, that George had already lost his freedom and that his alcoholism was going to kill him. The judge could deprive him of his liberty only to save his life, and that is what had happened.

George was stunned. He realized that alcoholism had taken away his freedom to choose, and the judge had taken away his liberty to save his life. He began to finally accept the path of recovery, A.A., and his need for God. Then I told him about the promise of a new freedom and a new happiness.

We don't have to make great big changes to have a new freedom and a new happiness. We can make little bitty changes that start to grow on us. For years and years, I had the plainest, drabbest clothes imaginable. I wore black slacks, white long-sleeve shirts, and black "Corfam" shoes. Corfam was a synthetic patent leather that never lost its shine and was impervious to water and dirt. My look never changed. It was drab and depressed, and I looked it. By the time I came to work at Hazelden, I had branched out a bit to khakis and both blue and white shirts, with ordinary black shoes that were not so shiny.

I really liked lecturing to patients, but I discovered that my 1:00 p.m. audience had 15 percent of the patients on withdrawal medications, 25 percent coming from relaxation exercises, and another 50 percent coming straight from lunch. My initial impression on them was "boring." I decided a little color might help, so I got some bright-red loafers and some bright-blue ones. I figured if the lecture was boring, they could always watch the shoes. Over time, people began to speculate on what kind of shoes I would have on that day, and I got brighter and brighter shoes. Today I've got some neon-blue patent-leather lace-ups from Louis Vuitton, and both blue and gold glitter slippers from Jimmy Choo. It's a lot of fun to play with the shoes and the patients.

I even had a pink-and-white-striped seersucker suit made for me in Hong Kong.

I once gave a talk to the governor and most of the legislature of Wyoming at the Governor's Awards Dinner for Mental Health and Chemical Dependency. When I walked in wearing my pink-striped seersucker suit and neon-blue shoes, they wondered if I was one of the crazy people from the mental health clinic, but I got a standing ovation at the end of my talk. I figured everybody wears a cowboy hat to Wyoming, so I might as well have fun and be different!

"We will not regret the past nor wish to shut the door on it."

Because the pain of my past was more than I could bear, I shut the door on it. I shut the door on it so firmly that it was gone. My mind broke into pieces, and the piece containing the memory of my past was not available—for my own protection. When keeping that piece separate turned against me in the form of a suicide wish, I had to accept that piece back into consciousness, which was very painful and difficult. This promise, that I would not regret the past, sounded like a spiteful joke.

I got practical advice from my sponsor, my meetings, and the pages of the Big Book. I got healing from friends, allies, a therapist, and God. Now I don't regret the past. I don't welcome the past. I just accept the past and allow myself the feelings that naturally come from it.

I don't wish to shut the door on it because I have learned that, in God's hands, the dark past will be at times the greatest possession I have in that it will be the key to life and happiness for others. With it, I can avert death and misery for them. My old self would bristle at that. I would have said it's unfair that my dark past could be the key to life and happiness for others, yet not bring happiness to me. That's not fair. However, I have learned to find joy in the ability to bring happiness to others.

I don't try to shut the door on the past because I think, in a way, we are all the people we have ever been. I am my five-year-old self, my ten-year-old self, my drunk college-student self, and my newly sober self—and we are all one. I need to accept myself, both as I am today and as I was in the past. To shut the door on the past would be to leave my five-year-old self out there, all alone.

Today I am writing this book, which I hope will be useful to others. Everything in my past, good and bad, has contributed to who I am today and has contributed to the ideas in this book. Without the past, these ideas would not be here to share with others.

We even find a way to let go of regret for the things we have done wrong. If we admit our wrongs and make amends—taking Steps Four through Nine—this process often gives us closer relationships with God and restored relationships with many of the people we have harmed in the past.

I used to regret being drunk through much of my academic career at Rutgers College and Princeton Theological Seminary. I used to regret all the things I imagined I would have learned if I had been sober during those years. Now, as I apply acceptance to those years, I am finding that I do remember some things from those schools. They were good schools, and I got something out of them, and that's enough. I contribute to their alumni funds, and have visited the campuses, and I wish them well in educating others. I don't regret the years I formerly regarded as lost.

"We will comprehend the word serenity and we will know peace."

Before I got into recovery, I thought the word *serenity* belonged in sappy greeting cards. My definition of peace was the same as Ambrose Bierce's in his nineteenth-century book *The Devil's Dictionary*: "Peace: A short period of preparation for the next war." If I had to pick a creature to identify with, it would have been an indignant porcupine.

Then, when I thought serenity was a possibility, I thought it would come when the situation changed. After a slow process of letting others alter my perception, I finally realized that serenity would come when I changed, even if the situation did not change.

The promise says, "And we will know peace." This meant nothing to me until it happened. I remember the first time I felt peace and happiness together. Priscilla and I were on vacation in Vienna. We had visited Saint Stephen's Cathedral in the center of the city. We went to a nearby Aida Café. Aida Cafés were kind of like the Dunkin' Donuts of Vienna. They were inexpensive cafés with pink Formica, pink tile walls, pink cash registers, and waitresses in pink dresses. They had many kinds of coffee and many pastries. The one we went to was a two-story shop, with bathrooms on the mezzanine between the floors. Priscilla had gone to the bathroom, and I was waiting for her at the top of the stairs. I was looking down on the first floor, at the people, the glass cases filled with pastries, the racks of newspapers, the reflections, and I felt peaceful and happy. I had never felt this before. It was as if the whole place lit up for me. I suddenly knew peace, and it just came to me, out of nowhere.

Today, there is a little sign in my office at Hazelden where patients can see it. It says, "Don't quit before the miracle happens." I don't know how to bring about happiness and peace; it just comes to us while we are practicing our program.

"No matter how far down the scale we have gone, we will see how our experience can benefit others."

It is our experience that makes us useful to others, along with our strength and our hope. I used to regard experience with cynicism because I regarded everything with cynicism. I said, "Experience is what you get when you didn't get what you wanted." That's partly true, but there is much more.

Human brains change over time. Beyond age fifty-five, we lose some of our mental acuity as the memory becomes less efficient. At the same time, the brain structure becomes more complex, which creates the opportunity to turn experience into wisdom. That is why, for example, fifty-five-year-olds are much more likely than eighteen-year-olds to lose their car keys but are much less likely to drive like jerks when they find them.

In recovery, we choose sponsors who have valuable experience we can use. We associate with peers we regard as wise. We invite "old timers" to speak at gatherings so we can benefit from their experience. When these experienced people speak, they do not tell us about their unbroken record of success. They tell us how far down they have gone, as well as what happened and what their lives are like now. They tell the whole story.

As we look at our whole stories and accept our whole lives—good and bad—we will come to understand how our experience can benefit others, and we share ourselves with others so we can be of service.

"That feeling of uselessness and self-pity will disappear."

My feeling of uselessness went away when I was a young adult. The feeling of self-pity lasted a lot longer. I grew up with the unshakable certainty that no one would ever love me, so I chose a path of becoming useful to ensure I would find a place in society based on my usefulness. I learned emergency medical service and fire fighting, and joined volunteer rescue squads and fire departments. In doing CPR I literally breathed life into three people. I rescued small children from burning homes.

I made it my business to know things. I read the *New York Times*, the *Wall Street Journal*, and a local paper every day, as well as several magazines and six or more online news sources. I have a huge amount of trivia stored in my head that occasionally becomes useful. I became good at problem solving so I would not feel useless.

The feeling of self-pity endured. It could not be cured or covered up by any amount of usefulness. It was a constant refrain of "poor me": "Poor me, anything I achieve will come to nothing." "Poor me, nothing will ever work." "Poor me, I will never be happy." "Poor me, I will never amount to anything." "Poor me, I will always be an outsider." "Poor me, poor me" became "Pour me a drink."

How did the "poor me's" disappear? The same way a headache disappears: slowly and without me noticing anything until they were gone. Somehow, through the alchemy of these Twelve Step programs, it all went away. Those feelings of uselessness and self-pity had disappeared.

"We will lose interest in selfish things and gain interest in our fellows."

It is a truly miserable trap to have low self-esteem, think poorly of ourselves, and also think we are the center of the universe. Only as alcoholics and addicts can we construct a trap in which we dislike ourselves, see no hope for the future, take drugs that make us more depressed, isolate ourselves from other people, and then become entirely self-centered so we can focus on the misery we have created.

I knew what I was doing—I was just powerless to change. I had joined the ego-protection program. I even joked about it. I would say, "I may not be much, but I'm all I think about!" or "Well, enough about me. How about you? What do YOU think about me?" My fellow alcoholics would laugh because they would recognize their own distorted egos in my jokes. Someone once asked me, "Have you ever been in love?" My smartass answer was, "Only with the sound of my own voice, thank God."

My alcoholic point of view was simple: I am always right. I was always right because I was the living *definition* of right. Whatever I said was right per se, because I had said it. These thoughts existed in the same mind that also thought I would never amount to anything. Confusing? Contradictory? Not if I was drinking or taking drugs, which I always was.

When my first sponsor asked me, "Are you willing to do what you're told?" he introduced me to the reality that there are other people in the world, and many of them knew better than me how to live. To recover, I had to stop listening only to the sound of my own voice. Through the Twelve Step programs, through listening to sane and sensible people, and through listening for the voice of God, I learned to lose interest in selfish things and gain interest in my fellows.

Now I live in a fascinating world. I now refer to my wife as "the Amazing Priscilla" because there is so much going on in her life that is just intriguing to me. I meet so many people during the week at work and in meetings that I cannot even keep track of them all, but every one of them has a story that is filled with hope and loss, struggle and triumph. I rarely watch television dramas about fictional people because I am so caught up in the stories of real people all around me.

I have adopted recovery as a great cause, worthy of my commitment. I am seeking it not just for me but for all of us. One of my slogans is, "I got drunk, but we got sober." I got into this mess of addiction on my own, but I can only recover in a group of drunks, a fellowship of recovering people.

"Self-seeking will slip away."

Self-seeking is the practice of sliding my selfishness back into an activity in a way that looks like it is intended to benefit others. Self-seeking is hard to voluntarily root out—the same way alcoholism is hard to voluntarily root out. It seems to be hard-wired into our brains, and addiction is a brain disease. We cannot entirely eliminate self-seeking, and yet the promise is that self-seeking will slip away.

Self-seeking happens when our disease undermines our good intentions. We might reach out to help another alcoholic, but only the alcoholic who is interesting or who might give us a job or a date or a ride. Self-seeking can be as minor as asking our spouse to go to a movie we really want to see, instead of sharing a list of the available movies and then telling him or her which one we'd like to see. Self-seeking can grow as large as founding a charity and then using it to give ourselves large paychecks that really belong in the private sector.

The cure for self-seeking lies both in our willingness to be cured and in a Power greater than ourselves. Self-seeking isn't removed by retraining. Self-seeking slips away as our love for others increases.

Dr. Silkworth attended to Bill Wilson in Towns Hospital many times. Most of what he knew about alcoholism was wrong, and the treatments failed again and again. Even so, Dr. Silkworth is a hero in A.A. and is known as "the little doctor who loved drunks." He was there to recognize the crucial change in Bill Wilson when Bill had his spiritual experience. Because Dr. Silkworth genuinely loved drunks, he could see that what happened to Bill Wilson was real, even though there was no scientific explanation for it.

As God gives us the love for other people that Dr. Silkworth had, our self-seeking just slips away. We don't see it slipping away. One day we notice it has left us. It returns from time to time, but it just doesn't have the power it once did.

"Our whole attitude and outlook upon life will change."

As with all the other changes that came upon us, this happened naturally. We have moved from dishonesty to honesty. When we had active addictions, we automatically hid them, and our answers were reflexive. We naturally said anything that drew attention away from the truth about us and the truth about out addictions. Over time we moved from addiction-centered, to self-centered, to other-centered, to God-centered. As the center of our lives moved, we naturally became more truthful. We no longer had any need to hide ourselves.

We moved from resentment to acceptance and from acceptance to gratitude. The stories of our lives did not change, but our whole attitude and outlook on our lives had been gradually changed by exposure to a new way of life. As we have been received and surrounded by members of a sympathetic and understanding fellowship, our burdens have been shared and ultimately healed.

Each time we move through the cycle of the Twelve Steps, we get more out of the steps—and out of the experience of traveling through the cycle together with men and women who are sharing what they have with us. Our understanding of the steps themselves grows deeper, our support for one another grows stronger, and our relationship with God and each other becomes more healing. If we complete the cycle a few times a year, then in ten, fifteen, or twenty years, we will have repeated the process and increased our benefits many times.

"Fear of people and of economic insecurity will leave us."

We might prefer this promise to be that economic insecurity itself would leave us, but this promise is that the *fear* of economic insecurity will leave us. Addiction teaches only one thing: it teaches us to fear. There is a "Jellinek Chart" of addiction and recovery, which is incorrectly attributed to E. M. Jellinek, MD. It was actually drafted by his students in his honor. The chart itself is quite revealing. One of the key elements identified in the chronic alcoholic is "vague indefinable fears."

I believe fear is an integral part of alcoholism and addiction. Part of our mind is terrified because we are dying of a relentless disease. Another part of our mind is censoring that knowledge, so the information we need about our own alcoholism and addiction is unavailable to us. It is censored by our own denial. The fear we are unable to feel has to go somewhere, so it attaches itself to whatever is available, until we are randomly afraid of all kinds of things. The most prominent things this indefinable fear attaches to are people and economic insecurity.

As we recover, our minds are less terrified of dying because we are not dying of our addictions any more. As the hidden terror of dying leaves our unconscious minds, the fear of people and of economic insecurity leaves us as well.

Economic insecurity left me long before the *fear* of economic insecurity left me. I have been saving and investing since I was twenty-six years old. I learned well the "rule of 72": money doubles in the amount of time represented by the interest rate divided into 72. The younger you start saving, the more powerful this leverage is. I've been running charts and graphs of net asset values and projected retirement income for decades. They did nothing to address my fear. Only as I learned to trust God through this program have I finally let go of that fear.

Because my fears ran unusually deep, way into my unconscious, I have looked for safe ways to unlearn fear. I had, years ago, learned to fly. I had gone on some "mystery adventures" with friends and with Priscilla, letting go of control.

Then, in 2011, I had a speaking engagement on a Friday night in New York City and then had the weekend free. New

York is my home, and I've done most of the usual tourist things, so I was looking online for things to do when I found a firm called Surprise Industries, which is in the surprise business. People sign up, individually or in small groups, and are taken somewhere in the city, blindfolded, for a surprise. The blindfolds come off to reveal the surprise.

I contacted them about getting an afternoon surprise in which I would let go and have the entire surprise conducted while I was blindfolded. They were happy to arrange it. So, I went to a café in Brooklyn where a waitress blindfolded me before I met my guide, who introduced herself as a fairy.

The story of the afternoon is a long one, but something special happened. We walked the streets of Brooklyn and talked for several hours with me blindfolded. At one point, we lay barefoot in soft grass in the shade in a park. The fairy said she would grant a wish, anything I wanted. I had fully committed to this fairyland experience, so I wished big. One bad result of remembering my abuse, during psychotherapy, was remembering the sound of my own screaming. Since then, for many years, I had been haunted by the sound. In my mind, my big fairy wish was for that sound to go away, but I didn't say the wish out loud.

We played in the park, ran through the sprinklers and got soaking wet on a hundred-degree day, and walked through a Hispanic street fair—all with me blindfolded. The fairy took me to an aerialist studio and had me climbing and swinging on silken ropes I could not see. When I finally grasped one silk rope and slid to the floor, I was surprised how high up I had been.

The afternoon ended, and we parted. The surprise was over. I hadn't felt any fear. I was glad I had been able to let go, trust, and enjoy myself. It was several days later that I noticed: the sound of my screams was gone, and it has not returned in the years since then.

"We will intuitively know how to handle situations which used to baffle us."

I hear people who are in Twelve Step programs telling me all the time, with surprise, how well they have handled new situations. They are pleased and amazed that they handled a sudden problem naturally and easily, finding the right answer on the spot, effortlessly, as if it had just been given to them. Often the right answer *had* just been given to them. I know, because there have been many times when the right answer has been just given to me.

The situations that traditionally baffle me are dealing with violent men and angry, scolding women. That is natural, since my sexual abuser was a violent man and my physical abuser was an angry, scolding woman. Situations that resemble my childhood abuse have had a tendency to throw me off my mental and emotional balance. That has gone away.

This promise tells us that we will intuitively know how to handle situations that used to baffle us. Again, this is not a study program of our own—it just comes to us as we make spiritual progress through the Twelve Steps and apply the traditions and spiritual principles of these programs to our lives. Here are two examples: one with a violent man and one with an angry woman.

AN INTUITIVE THOUGHT WITH A VIOLENT BUT REPENTANT MAN

I had a patient several years ago who was scheduled to do his Fifth Step with me. Fifth Steps are legally privileged in Minnesota and entirely private. People can confess crimes, and those crimes are not reportable. From my patient's story as he had shared it with his peers, I suspected he had killed people as part of his role in a drug-distribution gang. At his Fourth Step orientation, I told him about the difference between truth and evidence. "I killed someone" would be the kind of truth that belonged in a Fifth Step. Giving the name of the person he killed and the date and place of the killing would be legal evidence, and it would not be a good idea to share that. One reason I did not want him to share evidence was that if he had a relapse and returned to working for the drug gang, I wouldn't want him to return and kill me to get rid of any evidence he had left behind. I explained all of this, and he understood.

He came to the Fifth Step and said, "This program won't work for me." I said this program can work for anyone. He said it couldn't because he had killed eight people and there was no way he could make amends for killing eight people. Even if he turned himself in and the state executed him, that was only one life, and it wouldn't balance out the eight lives he had taken. Since he couldn't make amends, he said he couldn't work this program.

I did what the Big Book suggests and asked God for an intuitive thought or an inspiration. Then I got one. I told my patient he lacked creativity. I asked him if he had an organ donor card. He didn't. I told him to get one. When he died, I said, we could strip him for spare parts. He might save two or more lives. I told him that, drug-free, he would be a healthy young man. Once a month, he could eat a steak dinner and give a pint of clean blood to the Red Cross. He might save several lives that way. I told him that, with all due respect, he had a somewhat terrifying appearance. If he joined Narcotics Anonymous and developed rock-solid recovery, he could carry an NA message into his local county jail once a month. I had every confidence that he would have the attention and respect of the prisoners. If people heard his NA message and acted on it, he might save some lives.

The fact was, I told him, he owed God eight lives, and it was time to start paying God back—and just keep on paying God back for the rest of his life and let God do the arithmetic. That patient completed a very thorough Fifth Step that day and left with a sense of hope, believing that he, too, had a future in this program of recovery. I got postcards a couple of times from him over the next few years, just to say he was clean and sober and carrying the NA message into jail.

AN INTUITIVE THOUGHT WITH AN ANGRY WOMAN

Priscilla and I were on vacation in Bhutan. It's a remote mountain kingdom that has remained relatively unchanged over the years. The culture is very different from our own, and I was trying to learn about it and be respectful as a visitor. I knew I should remove my shoes and hat in a temple. I knew I should remove my hat outdoors in a temple courtyard. I was unaware that if people put up wooden stakes and colored rope in a square outdoors at a festival, that counted the same as a temple courtyard, even if there was no temple, and I shouldn't wear a hat.

We arrived late at a festival celebrating the return of the black-necked cranes to the town of Gangtey. We were late because two potato trucks had crashed, blocking the only road, and we walked the last half mile. I didn't notice that the men weren't wearing hats, and I sat down next to Priscilla in the fourth row.

A woman who looked and sounded like a white American turned and hissed at me to take my hat off, and I quickly did. She then went on to denounce me for everything that has ever been done wrong by white American men, beginning with Columbus. She went on about the destruction of the Plains Indians, the building of the transcontinental railroad, the importation of poor Chinese people to work the California gold mines, the annexation of Mexico, the Spanish-American War, World War I and the use of mustard gas, the stock-market crash of 1929, the bombing of Hiroshima…until I lost track.

It was a rapid-fire monologue, and my mind drifted. I thought, *Maybe she's Canadian. They look and sound like us. She's certainly angry at American men.* I looked at my watch. The entire rant took only about six minutes, but that's a long time when somebody really hates you. I kept thinking, *Maybe I'm supposed to learn something here*, but I couldn't think of what it was. Finally she stopped.

I paused for an intuitive thought. Then I spoke: "I do regret wearing my hat where it was not appropriate, and I hope you notice that I did remove it when challenged. But I want you to know that I am actually here for a deeper and a more spiritual reason."

"What possible spiritual reason could you have to be here?" she spat out.

"Oh," I said, "I am the embodiment of all your resentments. And no matter where you go in the world, you cannot escape me." After a moment of stunned silence, she got up and left.

What I said actually was true. She didn't know me well enough to justify her hatred. The hatred she had came from within her. As for me, instead of going away feeling guilty, I felt untroubled by the whole thing, except for wearing the hat in the wrong place.

"We will suddenly realize that God is doing for us what we could not do for ourselves."

What could we do for ourselves? We could drink and drug for ourselves. We could fight for ourselves. We could try and try again for ourselves. We could make excuses for ourselves. We could place blame for ourselves. We could rationalize our failures for ourselves. We could put on a brave, false front all by ourselves.

On my own, I could only quit drinking. God and these Twelve Step programs have made me sober. On my own, I could rent drinking buddies by buying rounds. God and these programs have given me friends. On my own, I somehow managed to hold on to a job, although it was getting harder. God and these programs have given me a calling. On my own, I ended up divorced. God has given me a happy marriage, and these programs have given me spiritual principles that have provided me with a way of life that works.

All of us, at whatever level of progress we currently enjoy, as we look over the progress we have made, need to be honest. Can we look at our progress and say, "We have done this all by ourselves"? I think not. All I really knew how to do when I entered this program was drink and drug. Everything else has been given to me as a gift, from those who have gone before me and from God.

PROMISES FULFILLED

When I first read these promises, I thought they were an exaggeration. I thought they were a product of hyperbole, rhetoric from the 1930s. Then one evening I was at a large meeting, and the group had a long introduction to the evening. They read the Preamble, the Twelve Steps, the Twelve Traditions, and the Promises, which conclude with this passage:

> *Are these extravagant promises? We think not. They are being fulfilled among us—sometimes quickly, sometimes slowly. They will always materialize if we work for them. (Alcoholics Anonymous, p. 84)*

When the reader got to the second sentence in that passage, the whole large group shouted, "WE THINK NOT." It startled me. They seemed delighted to shout it out. It sounded like an act of defiance. Many of them looked as if they didn't have much money. Many had what I call that "high-mileage look" of people on whom addiction has taken a physical toll. And yet they were defiant and happy when they shouted, "We think not," in response to the question, "Are these extravagant promises?"

It turns out that they are not extravagant promises. At five years sober, *some* of them had come true for me. At ten years sober, *most* of them had come true for me. At fifteen years sober, *all* of them had come true for me. Are these extravagant promises? I think not. Even after all the promises come true, they become more and more true as the years go on.

Now I have become happier than I could have possibly imagined. I cannot fully explain it, so I offer just one more story. It is from January 2011.

On January 24, 2011, Priscilla and I had been married exactly thirty-five years. I was then sixty-two years old, and she was seventy-three. I had been sober for twenty-two years, and all the promises had come true. We were having dinner in the Oriental Hotel in Bangkok, our favorite city hotel in the world, on the outdoor terrace by the river.

It's a beautiful spot: a white marble terrace with a white marble railing and black wrought-iron lamp posts topped with white globes. There were little white lights in the bushes. We had a table right by the Chao Phraya River, which is the main street of Bangkok, with all the local and ocean-going ships nearby.

There, at our anniversary dinner, I gave her a love letter I had written that day on hotel stationery. When you write a letter with an open heart, it sometimes takes on a life of its own. On the fifth page, it took a turn, and I wrote:

It is, ultimately, a gratitude letter. You are the most important person in my life because you were chosen by God to bring me into whom I was supposed to be.

You remember: I've always said that I was attracted to you because you were both good and kind. You didn't expect that I would be interested in you as a date because I was 10 years younger. I was drawn to what I most needed, without knowing why.

You have been a steady influence, thirty-five years of dinners are like water on rock. Eventually there is a graceful curve resulting.

Even when I am not listening, I cannot avoid being changed by who you are. Your goodness and kindness are real. I knew that from the beginning, and I have had the full benefit of you for thirty-five years.

I love you and I always will.

Yours truly, John

Priscilla hasn't changed much over the years, but I have. The experience of being married to her has been a lot like water on stone, and I have become smooth and, literally, round. I've been married to her for a long time, but for a long time, I didn't get the benefit of our marriage. I didn't benefit because my capacity for love was limited, first by abuse and trauma, then by alcoholism and addiction, and then by the limits of my rigid personality. God, the fellowship of Alcoholics Anonymous, and Priscilla have given me the capacity to love that I never had; and so I love life and love her so much more now than ever before because, at long last, I can—and I am happy.

*****Keep Coming Back. It Works!*****

ABOUT THE AUTHOR

John MacDougall was born in New York City in 1949. He graduated from Rutgers College, a division of Rutgers, the State University of New Jersey in New Brunswick, New Jersey, in 1972. He graduated with a master of divinity degree from Princeton Theological Seminary in Princeton, New Jersey, in 1976. He graduated from the Drew University Theological School in Madison, New Jersey, in 1985, with a doctor of ministry degree with a focus in family therapy. He is the coauthor, with Bowen White, MD, of *Clinician's Guide to Spirituality*, published in 2001 by McGraw-Hill and Hazelden.

John was ordained as a minister in the United Methodist Church in 1976 in Ocean City, New Jersey, and served churches in Riverside and Paulsboro, New Jersey; in the Mascoma Valley Parish in and near Enfield, New Hampshire; and in Everett, Massachusetts, for eighteen years before beginning his specialized ministry at Hazelden in 1994.

John married Priscilla in 1976, and they have two daughters, Priscilla Anderson and Chris Lopez. They have three grandchildren, Sawyer Anderson, Ana Lopez, and Macky Lopez. They are grateful for happy family relationships with their daughters, sons-in-law, and grandchildren.

John enjoys speaking at A.A. events and has spoken at A.A. Roundups in Aspen, Colorado, and Las Vegas and Reno, Nevada. He has spoken to Hazelden alumni groups around the country, to the International Doctors in A.A., and to many other groups interested in recovery. He can be contacted at mail@johnmacdougall.net and his author website is www.johnmacdougall.net.

Made in the USA
Lexington, KY
20 November 2013